THEMES IN ORTHODOX PATRISTIC PSYCHOLOGY

Volume One

HUMILITY

By

Archimandrite Chrysostomos

with
The Reverend Theodore M. Williams
and
Sister Paula

Prologue by Mother Alexandra

CENTER FOR TRADITIONALIST
ORTHODOX STUDIES

Library of Congress Catalog Card No.
82-74509

Copyright 1983 by
CENTER FOR TRADITIONALIST
ORTHODOX STUDIES

About the Author

The Very Rev. Chrysostomos, B.A., B.A., M.A., M.A., Ph.D. (Princeton), has served as Abbot of the St. Gregory Palamas Monastery since 1978. A small dependency of the Holy Monastery of Sts. Cyprian and Justina in Fili (Athens), Greece, the Monastery was moved from Hayesville, Ohio, in early 1983, to rural Northern California, seeking greater isolation and a more cloistered monastic life. Father Chrysostomos subsequently relinquished all but formal supervision of the community to its present superior and has dedicated his efforts to the scholarly work of the Center for Traditionalist Orthodox Studies, which he directs.

From 1972 to 1975, Father Chrysostomos was a preceptor in the department of psychology at Princeton University. In 1975, after resigning his post as assistant professor of psychology at the University of California, Riverside, he entered the monastic life. He was raised to the rank of Archimandrite in 1978. Father Chrysostomos held the posts of associate professor of psychology at Ashland College from 1980 to 1983, and adjunct assistant professor in Christian thought at Ashland Theological Seminary from 1979 to 1983. Formerly a visiting scholar at The Divinity School, Harvard University, he spends the greater part of his time at his monastic Mother House in Greece.

About the Contributors

The Rev. Theodore M. Williams is a graduate of the U.S. Naval Academy (Annapolis). He received his B.A. degree in philosophy from Georgia State University, the B.D. degree from the School of Theology, University of the South, and his doctorate in theology from Emory University. From 1976 to 1981, Father Theodore taught theology, Eastern Church history, and Greek in the Graduate School of Theology, Oral Roberts University. Ordained to the married Priesthood in the Antiochian Archdiocese in 1980, he was received into the Old Calendar Church of Greece a year later and now serves the St. Gregory Palamas Monastery.

Sister Paula (Reid) received her B.A. degree (magna cum laude) in English and creative writing from Ashland College, where she was a college scholar. She is a sister of the Skete of St. Xenia, in Wildwood, California, a monastic house of the Russian Orthodox Church Outside Russia.

ALSO BY ARCHIMANDRITE CHRYSOSTOMOS

The Ancient Fathers of the Desert
  (Hellenic College Press, 1980)

Orthodox Liturgical Dress: An Historical Treatment
  (Holy Cross Orthodox Press, 1981)

Contemporary Eastern Orthodox Thought:
The Traditionalist Voice
  with Hieromonk Auxentios and Hierodeacon Akakios
  (Nordland House Publishers, 1982)

Scripture and Tradition: A Comparative Study of the
Eastern Orthodox, Roman Catholic, and Protestant Views
  with Hieromonk Auxentios
  (Nordland House Publishers, 1982)

Orthodoxy and Papism
  (Center for Traditionalist Orthodox Studies, 1983)

DEDICATION

I wish to dedicate this small volume to my forebears. My family hails from Spain and Greece, from two wholly different traditions with ultimately common roots. From my Spanish heritage, from a family of some historic import, I have received a pride which, as a monk, humbles me. From my Orthodox Greek background, I have gained a vision of humility that awes me. In my faults and my aspirations, therefore, I have in a sense brought together that which has been so long separated. May my efforts, however unsuccessful, inspire all true Orthodox, both in the East and the West, and justify me to my forefathers.

I would also like this book to stand as an inadequate tribute to a spiritual brother, the Priest-monk David, who, throughout trials, illness, and the burden of slander brought upon him by those "perfect in their faith," has made his loyalty to the Church a perfect statement of true humility.

ACKNOWLEDGEMENTS

In writing a book of this sort, which touches on one of the most important and personal traits of the Orthodox spiritual aspirant, there are naturally many people whom one would wish to acknowledge. However, there are so many who have touched my own spiritual life in their abundant acts of humility, that I could not possibly hope to thank each of them. I will therefore thank them all by an expression of gratitude for the examples of humility set before me by two individuals: my spiritual Father, Bishop Cyprian (Metropolitan of Oropos and Fili), who personifies humility; and another of His Eminence's spiritual sons, Hieromonk Ambrosios, who practices, in his *daily* behavior, a humility which I could only hope to claim as my *ultimate* goal.

The daily operation of a monastery leaves little time for such things as writing. The fact that I have such time prompts me to thank those around me for their extra duty, in the face of the time which I have taken away from what would otherwise be my own duties. In this respect, the Reverend Father Theodore Gacanin and his wife, Prebytera Nadezhda, have been of unselfish assistance to the monastery. I sincerely thank them. Of more indirect, though no less appreciated, aid have been Mr. and Mrs. Louis Lekas, valued friends of the monastery. I thank them with equal sincerity.

Much of the writing of this book was completed in the summer of 1981 with the support of a Chairman's Grant from the National Endowment for the Humanities. For securing this funding, I am deeply grateful for the assistance of Mr. John Staurski, administrative aid to Senator Howard Metzenbaum of Ohio, and of Dr. Joseph Duffey, former Chairman of the NEH.

Archimandrite Chrysostomos
Mid-Pentecost 1982

CONTENTS

PROLOGUE

By Mother Alexandra
formerly Her Royal Highness, Ileana
Princess of Romania and Archduchess of Austria

"The meek shall inherit the earth;
and shall delight themselves in the
abundance of peace" (Psalm 37:11)

Humility, like faith, is a gift of Grace. Some happy souls may, perhaps, be disposed toward it at birth; but all, whatever their dispositions, have to struggle with pride and self-satisfaction. Rare, indeed, would be the person who does not enjoy praise and admiration, for taking pride in a job well done is a very human trait and need not even be sinful, as such. The truly humble man, however, is he who is immune to both flattery and offense, who, as Kipling says, ". . . can meet with triumph and disaster / And treat those two imposters just the same." Accepting all with equanimity, this man quietly follows his path to salvation, while "delighting," as the Psalmist says, "in the abundance of peace."

But what does humility really mean? The derivation of the word "humble" is the Latin "humus," meaning "soil," and herein lies a most apt metaphor for understanding what is most basic to humility. The humble feel themselves equal to the soil upon which they walk and from which they are made. They cannot be lowered, for they are already low. But this lowliness in no way means servility; it means purity and godliness. Satan's great fall came from his inordinate pride, which rendered him impure. For us, each time that we let pride get the better of us, we have similarly soiled ourselves. This is the nature of our lowliness: not servility, but a purity shared with the soil, by which we paradoxically remain unsoiled (by pride).

It is a curious fact, too, that the more humble we become, the closer we are to God. Our Lord Jesus Christ said that, unless we become as children, we cannot enter the Kingdom of Heaven. We must, therefore, become simple and pure, like children, to draw near God. And the source of this purity, says St. John Cassian, is unavailable to us "unless we have acquired real humility of heart." The ascent to God, the climb toward the divine, begins with the acquisition of humility. We approach the heights by attaining lowliness. We acquire spiritual maturity by becoming children.

It is important to understand clearly that humility lies not primarily in the natures with which we are born, but in how we develop those natures. The decisions which we ultimately make in life determine who we are. We are not responsible for what talents we may have, as also we are not responsible for what happens to us in the world's turmoil. What we are responsible for is what we do with what we have and what we make of what happens to us. Thus, those who are called to high stations in life can be humble in their hearts, while a sweeper can feel envy and pride. Haughtiness can dwell equally in the heart of the mighty one and in the beggar. The attainment of humility rests outside the rank and station to which one is born; it resides in what we do with what we are. In the eyes of God, all men are equal, and we are judged accordingly, not by our rank, but by our accomplishments.

What we must all do, then, is develop the degree of natural humility with which we are born, whether it be great or small. We must nurture it, perhaps even forcing ourselves to act humbly, no matter how difficult that may be to do. In time, what we act may become reality. We must be cautious in our actions and our deeds and in our habits, remembering the task before us: the acquisition of humility. Clearly our own wills are involved here, and whether we humble or exalt ourselves depends greatly on our own volition. It is only the result of our willful humility or pride which lies outside our grasp — in the divine promise of the Saviour: "Whoever shall exalt himself shall be abased; and he that shall humble himself shall be exalted" (Matt. 23:12).

And what of this humility? What does it profit us? Above all, true humility shows itself in the most glowing colors when we are beset by adversity. It is our only hope in the inevitable bleakness of human life. When adversity strikes, we can meekly bow our heads in acceptance, without outward complaint or inward revolt. We can remember always that Jesus, the master of the most extreme humility, during his trial gave hardly any answers. And he asks that we pick up our crosses and likewise follow him. "Take my yoke," he beckons, "and learn from me; I am gentle and humble of heart: and you shall find rest for your souls. For my yoke is easy and my burden is light" (Matt. 11:29-30). Indeed, if we let these words guide us and follow the example set by Christ before us, our spirits will be strong and we will humbly endure all things in love. Humility guides us to the Spirit, the fruits of which are "love, joy, peace, long-suffering, gentleness, faith, meekness, and temperance . . ." (Gal. 5:22-23). Humility engenders meekness, against which no earthly law, no persecution, and no adversity can prevail.

The Holy Fathers from the earliest times dwell on humility, and Holy Scripture abounds in emphasis of its great virtue. The subject which Father Chrysostomos has chosen for his present book reaches, therefore, into the inner core of Christianity. It is an essential subject, resounding from the past and necessarily heard in the present. These sounds should not prompt in us abstract thought or mere reflection, but humble submission to the Will of God: "Humility consists not in considering our *conscience, but in recognizing God's Grace and compassion"* (St. Mark the Ascetic). *Humility, as we said in our opening words, is — in recognition of our efforts and as a reward for our love of God — a free gift given by Grace.*

Orthodox Monastery of the Transfiguration
Ellwood City, Pennsylvania
The Dormition Fast, 1981

INTRODUCTION

The present volume is the first in a series of projected volumes on themes in the psychology of the Fathers of the Eastern Orthodox Church. In general, the themes will parallel the major topical divisions in the primary collection of writings on the early Eastern monastics of the Egyptian desert, the *Euergetinos* [Εὐεργετινός]. The *Euergetinos,* first published in the eighteenth century through the efforts of two Greek Saints, Makarios of Corinth and Nikodemos of the Holy Mountain, recounts the lives and spiritual accomplishments of the early desert Fathers. These ascetic strugglers, during the first few centuries of Christianity, brought the Christian virtues into a living witness. Their lives reveal a practical application of the theory of Christianity, and it is from their witness that centuries of Christians, both in the East and in the West, have drawn their very definitions of the Christian life, the Christian soul, and the Christian mind. Their exploits and deeds, as narrated in the *Euergetinos,* form a brilliant mosaic, a composition patterned by such singular virtues as humility, obedience, repentance, and love, among others. From these virtues we will draw the themes for the individual volumes in our series, psychological pieces that might ultimately lead us to a vision of the φρόνημα τῶν Πατέρων , of that resplendent mosaic which is the mind of the Fathers themselves. Accordingly, each volume will build on translated selections from the various topical divisions of the *Euergetinos,* tracing from the early desert to contemporary Orthodox spirituality the golden thread of continuity by which the Orthodox Fathers, past and present, are joined " ἐν τῷ αὐτῷ νοΐ " ["in the same mind"] and " ἐν τῇ αὐτῇ γνώμῃ " ["in the same thought"] (I Corinthians 1:10).

To initiate an English-language series on the psychology of the Orthodox Fathers is an onerous task.

1

Western thinkers are accustomed to separating the mind and the spirit. If they study humility, obedience, repentance, or even love, they treat these subjects either from the perspective of the spirit, phenomenologically, or in a behavioristic way, from the perspective of the mind (or, more precisely, of the brain). Modern psychology, for example, rarely posits a nexus between the mind and the spirit and most sedulously eschews the world of phenomenology, of the spirit. To be sure the rare exceptions exist and are as venerable as William James, as celebrated as Carl Jung, and as timely as Viktor Frankl. But these men, to a large extent, are the *bêtes noires* of today's psychology, at best thought of as eclectic eccentrics, at worst as alchemist-like charlatans. For the most part, such things as humility, obedience, repentance, or love are reduced to specific, observable behaviors ("operationalized" in scientific parlance) and studied as variables shaped by the environment, social conditioning, or perhaps the personality. They are separated from the spirit, indeed from the soul, and lose a certain wholeness. Even from the standpoint of the *Gestalt* psychologists, who strive to find a wholeness in the person, this wholeness is more perceptual or cognitive than spiritual; the mind dominates.

The Orthodox Fathers, on the other hand, know of no such separation of the mind and spirit. If one attains to the spiritual virtues, it is through the interaction and cooperation of mind and spirit. True psychology, for them, is not the simple description of habituation, of the reinforcement patterns by which the mind blindly reacts to stimuli in the environment — though, as in the case of St. John of the Ladder, they knew this limited sense of psychology to a degree that would astound a contemporary learning theorist. True psychology is the control of the mind's sensitivity to the environment by the mind's harmonious cooperation with the spirit. It encompasses, moreover, the entire process by which the spirit, too, is touched by the world, and by which the spirit frees itself from its fallen state and comes to interact in concord with the Will of God. The Orthodox Fathers understand psychology, in short, for what it truly is: ψυχολογία , the study of the soul.

Western thinkers are at times wont to underestimate the actuality of the wholeness of mind and spirit that, for the Orthodox Fathers, constitutes the person. They fail to grasp that at the very core of Orthodox spirituality lies the potential for the most intimate communion of the worlds of the spirit and the mind (indeed, in a limited way, the flesh), culminating in θέωσις [*theosis,* divinization], or participation, in the present life, of the human in the divine. As Professor Joan Hussey, the eminent Byzantinist, has commented, the Orthodox Church approaches the heavenly through the earthly, through the material, and (we might add) attempts to bring them into harmony. Humility, obedience, repentance, and love, therefore, are not, for the Orthodox, simple virtues or mere human attributes conditioned by various environmental or psychic factors alone; they are, rather, elements in a larger psychological scheme, in which the individual undergoes a transformation in mind and spirit. They are more than the characteristics defined in the limited psychology of the modern West. They are special virtues which derive from both the inner and the outer worlds of man, both from his mind and from his spirit. Their significance rests in that special, mystical psychology of the Fathers, the consensus of mind and thought captured so uniquely in Orthodox Tradition.

We see that the psychology of the Orthodox Fathers, far more complex and expansive than the psychologies of contemporary social scientists, frightfully challenges the limitations of the Western intellect, truncated as that intellect is by its mentalistic and spiritualistic poverty. This is especially true for Western converts to Eastern Orthodoxy and for Christians born into the Orthodox

Church but raised in the West. They intuitively realize, when they are painfully honest with themselves, that the Orthodox world of the spirit, in the Orthodox theological system, is integrally bound up with the world of the Orthodox mind. To be Orthodox is not just to hold a belief; it is to have a psychology, a peculiar psychology which blends what one believes with the way that one behaves and thinks. It becomes suddenly apparent, in the process of honest self-analysis, that Orthodox belief and Western behavior and patterns of thinking are not fundamentally compatible.

The Westerner, whether Orthodox or not, must come finally to understand that an acceptance of Orthodox belief is an acceptance of an Orthodox way of thinking, of an Orthodox psychology which formed the great Orthodox empires of Byzantium and Holy Russia, among others. He must come to the sometimes disconcerting conclusion that, despite the inevitable limitations of these Orthodox societies (which polemical heterodox writers have exploited at the cost of the tremendous accomplishments of the empires), they represent the blending of spirit and mind, lifted to the level of the blending of religion and culture, which is the psychology of the Fathers. With this realization there often comes an immediate repulsion, the Westerner musing: "Must I give up my own culture to be Orthodox?" And as often as not, this repulsion gives way to an accusation of philetism against those who properly exalt the classical model of Orthodox society epitomized in the Byzantine and Russian empires. The repulsion prompts a distorted understanding of the principle of accommodation to diverse cultures which is a touchstone of the Orthodox missionary tradition.

This misunderstanding is a further failure to grasp the psychology of the Fathers. Just as the mind and the spirit cannot be separated, so religion and culture, in the Orthodox *Weltanschauung*, cannot be separated. Virtues are formed by the harmonious interaction of the mind and the spirit, guided by the Divine Will. So, too, a worldly society is exalted and transformed when its culture and religion reflect the Divine Will. As alien as such a concept may be to those whose notion of theocracy is limited to the Papacy or Calvin's Geneva, this reflection is, after all, the triumph towards which every Orthodox society has striven. This reflection is the image of the icon of the earthly realm ascending toward the archetype of the heavenly city. The cultures of the Orthodox Fathers were the *joint expressions of their minds,* just as the Church, in the great Orthodox empires, was the *joint expression of their spirits,* the true ἐκκλησία .

Where this psychology prevails, whether among Greeks, Russians, Serbs, or (perhaps eventually) Americans, it transcends nationality and culture as we commonly understand them. It is a deep expression of Orthodoxy itself, and it is incumbent upon us that we honor and emulate this cultural psychology. It calls us to a vision of the heavenly homeland, moving us away from the mundane into conformity with the spiritual. We give up a culture which is not truly a culture for an internal spiritual sense, for a transformed view of society, for a *spiritual culture,* as it were. And this is not for us philetism, for philetism exalts the worth of the societies of man, seducing us, in our love for them, to ask if we "must give up our own culture to be Orthodox." To know the psychology of an Orthodox society is to know an elemental force in the spiritual evolution of all mankind. It is to enter a realm where philetism cannot be.

It is to no small extent that we see in contemporary Orthodoxy in the West — and, one might venture to say, even to a limited degree in the East, as in the xenophilous fervor of many young intellectuals in Greece today — not only a misunderstanding of the encompassing psychology of the Fathers, but a vehement resistance to it. A new convert to Eastern Orthodoxy, for example, finding little significance in some of the "externals" of more traditional Orthodox worship, recently wrote a friend referring to these liturgical traditions as a preoccupation with "bells and smells." Undoubtedly the writer's feelings were expressed with sincerity and honesty. However, they betray an internal resistance to the notion that the ritualistic practices of the Church transmit, through the transformation of the mind (indeed, of the senses, even the olfactory and acoustic senses), a spiritual perception; i.e., an awareness of a psychology of ritual, of a psychology in this realm too (that of worship), formed in classical Orthodox societies and passed down by them to those of us in the West.

In this same vein, some Orthodox in America, in what is a shameful display of poor taste, have derided the Bishops of the Russian Orthodox Church Abroad (the Russian Synod first formed in Karlovtzy, under the protection of the Serbian Patriarchate, by Prelates fleeing the Communist onslaught) for including, among the newly glorified martyrs of Russia under the Communist yoke, the Tsar Nicholas II and his family. Amidst vulgar accusations against the "White Russian Synod," as it has been insolently called, these captives of a Western mentality have impugned the sanctity of the Tsar and his family and the very reality of their massacre for reasons of faith — something reminiscent of the less vocal, albeit popular, attacks against the holiness of St. Constantine the Great. The notion that, because he was not (in the opinion of some) an exemplary ruler, the Tsar could not be a Saint is one of the more ludicrous arguments put forth in these attacks. It should not be imagined, of course, that political aptitude is a prerequisite for spiritual eminence. The more basic question in this dispute, however, stems again from a misunderstanding of the cultural psychology of traditional Orthodoxy.

There can be, by definition, no mere "political" act in

a traditional Orthodox society, for society and the spiritual are intimately joined. There exists not even the possibility of *la vie spirituelle* in the Western sense, separated as it is from other aspects of social reality. Hence, a political assassination is not the simple murder of a ruler; it is an act of violence against the spiritual fibre of society. And who can doubt this in recounting the savage barbarism surrounding the death of the Tsar-Martyr Nicholas and his family? The atrocious viciousness of their murderers calls to mind an attack against all decency, against every moral principle with which religion itself, whether Eastern or Western, is aligned. Just as St. Constantine, who brought peace to the Church, was a pivotal figure in the propagation of the Christian message across the Roman Empire, so the last Russian Tsar, in ruling over the last, great Orthodox empire, over one sixth of earth's land mass, fulfilled his role, even unto death, according to the Divine Will. One emperor ushered in the age of the Orthodox empire, the other ushered it out. And history, as the fulfillment of God's Will, elevates both of them above human views of moral perfection or spiritual attainment. They belong to a realm of holiness not fully within the scope of our limited human reason to understand. History vindicates them, because of their singular import in the unfolding of Orthodox society, of any human frailty. How much more they are innocent of the accusations placed before them by those who fail to understand the basic nature of Patristic psychology both at the individual and cultural levels.

Even the supposed "cultural oddities" of the classical Orthodox societies are at times nothing less than remnants of the Patristic psychology bequeathed to them by their forebears. Here, too, one must not succumb to a superficial view of these traits, as though they were simple "cultural differences." In his brilliant, evocative study of Gandhi, the renowned psychologist, Erik Erikson, seeks within Gandhi's spiritual life and religious heritage the source of the Indian leader's personality. This is the same course which we must pursue in investigating the Orthodox world. So encompassing is the Orthodox ethos, that one can boldly assert that the individual, in that world, does not much affect the spiritual milieu in which he lives; rather, the religious life in a classical Orthodox society forms and operates on the man. Orthodox man derives from his religion, not his religion from him. Thus many ostensible cultural traits are in actual fact expressions of profound theological principles which operate in the social and political realities of everyday Orthodox life. Let me illustrate my point.

In reference to the expansive nature of classical Indian religion, Professor Erikson notes that Indians are often characterized as pathological liars, devoid of a sense of personal honesty as we in the West understand it. Rather than attribute this, in the simplistic manner of most social psychologists, to social conditioning or to a peculiarity in the moral development of Indians, he turns to Indian religious philosophy. In traditional Hindu thought, the notion of truth has always been a metaphysical one, lifted away from the locus of human interaction and personal attributes. The apparent penchant for lying among Indians, then, in Dr. Erikson's mind, results from a concept of truth which permeates the culture and the personality. To think, when an Indian lies, that he is operating from an indifference to the truth is an unjustified and rather unfair assumption. In fact, it is out of a deference for a truth not present in such metaphysical dimensions in Western society that the Indian often fails to emphasize personal honesty.

Orthodox, too, in a traditional society, would, while extolling the virtue of personal honesty, emphasize that truth is ultimately a subtle, spiritual quality, transcending the individual and the limitations of his personal psychology. At times this gives forth to less preoccupation with personal honesty. Thus pejorative terms related to classical Orthodox societies have entered into the Western vocabulary. As often as one hears of "Byzantine intrigue," he hears of the slyness of the Russian character and the general deceptiveness of the Eastern European. While these accusations are, on the whole, fatuous accusations, as such, and certainly clear examples of cultural intolerance by those who repeat them, it is by no accident that they relate to populations nurtured in the bosom of the Eastern Church. They represent, in their distorted and accusatory way, an acknowledgement of the wholly unique manner in which Orthodox life is conducted. They aver that the Western idea of truth is, just as when applied to the Indian East, inadequate to capture the psychology of the Orthodox East.

In my own experimental investigations as a layman and psychologist, I conducted studies which brought the question of cultural disparity and spiritual psychology into vivid focus for me. I came to understand that, in the Orthodox personality, the blending of mind and spirit is observable even in cognitive processes and overt behaviors. In a series of publications, the distinguished Russian émigré psychologist, Professor Nikolai Khokhlov, and I have presented data that establish, with some certainty, that Greek populations tolerate far greater ambiguity in their cognitions than Western European and American subjects. There have always been, of course, acknowledged differences in the ways that different nationalities approach their psychological worlds. The Germans show a certain disposition toward order and consistency *(Ordnung und Festigkeit)* that can be demonstrated by psychometric means. The Spanish, on the other hand, seem to tolerate some inconsistency, as evidenced by a traditional Spanish proverb: "Si una persona no se contradice, quizás es porque no tiene nada que decir" ["If a person does not contradict himself, perhaps it is because he has nothing to say"]. But these divergent views are more literary and poetic, in the final analysis, since both Germans and Spaniards, in empirical investigations, show the consistency in cognitions which is taken by most social psychologists as a cornerstone of social, if not sensory, perception. Dr. Khokhlov and I found, however, that our Greek subjects tolerated ambiguity at a deep cognitive level, that they have a psychology, perhaps, not predicated on cognitive consistency. And preliminary data seem to suggest that this finding holds for other traditionally Orthodox populations.

In the Orthodox theological world, one might speak of a kind of relative absolutism. What is an absolute manifestation of truth in the spiritual realm is not always understood in absolute categories in the mundane world. For instance, the idea of the Trinity (fundamentally a theological formulation of the Eastern Fathers), while a dogmatic absolute in spiritual terms, may only be relatively understood by the categories of human reason. Consequently, no traditional Orthodox finds difficulty in preserving and protecting the precise form of the dogmatic, theologic explication of the Holy Trinity by the Holy Fathers, while at the same time acknowledging his own inability even to fathom the nature of this truth. All Orthodox theological terms, indeed, have reference to multiple dimensions, to multiple planes of spiritual experience and insight. The same expressions and words can, at times, refer to several different phenomena, depending on the intent of the writer and the skill and spiritual development of the reader. Tolerance of ambiguity, then, is part of the spiritual life of the Eastern Christian, part of the psychology passed down by the Fathers, which acts both on the mind and the spirit. A supposed cultural oddity, by which Orthodox populations seem to tolerate cognitive inconsistency, is not that at all; it is an expression of a psychology perhaps necessary to an understanding of the sublime, abstract realm in which Orthodox theologizing takes place — a psychology which touches both the mind and the spirit and which we must attain, to some extent, in order to reach into the inner core of the Christian Truth as Orthodox receive it. To resist this psychology is to court spiritual peril.

We have acknowledged the difficulties involved in an exposition of Orthodox Patristic psychology for a Western readership. The Western intellectual understands psychology, the person, society, culture, and religion in a way that is foreign to the world of Eastern Christian thought. Moreover, as we have pointed out, even Orthodox Christians living in the West have estranged themselves from the thinking of their forefathers. They have at times, in fact, developed attitudes inimical to the classical Orthodox world. As challenging as these impediments may be to an understanding of the psychology of the Orthodox Fathers, however, they are secondary in the face of the great silence, the great historical amnesia, in the West vis-à-vis the Orthodox Church and the historical road of the Christian religion. Despite the presence of many millions of Orthodox Christians in the West, and despite the fact that Orthodox scholars of singular fame have held forth in some of the most prestigious academic institutions in America and Western Europe, there is still a dearth of knowledge concerning the Eastern Orthodox Church. This lack of knowledge, as we shall see, is both innocent and intentional.

At the popular level, knowledge of the Orthodox Church has simply not reached all Westerners. One of the Fathers of our monastery, speaking to a Protestant women's guild about the Eastern Christian tradition, was astounded when, during the question period following his lecture, a woman in the audience asked, "Does your Church use our Bible?" The questioner was equally surprised by the response: "No, actually you use a translation of ours." This episode captures the enigmatic

11

situation of the Orthodox Church in the West. Christianity is an Eastern religion. It was spread, initially, in Eastern tongues. Monasticism, the early liturgies, the basic dogmatic formulations of the Christian Faith, the earliest canon of Scripture — all of these are basically of Eastern origin. The Eastern Orthodox Church is, as one Western authority puts it, the "Mother Church," Christianity's oldest Church. Yet a Roman Catholic living in the West is astonished, if not a bit insulted, to learn that there is a Christian Church with traditions that outdate the traditions of his own religion. Protestants, the champions of the Reformation principle of *sola Scriptura,* are aghast to find that the Orthodox Church considers the canon of Scripture a product of Her ecclesiastical tradition and spiritual domain. The enigma of the alienation of the Christian West from the Christian East is captured in one of Pascal's aphorisms: "How many kingdoms know nothing of us!" It is at once the complaint of the misunderstood Eastern Christian and the apology of newly-informed Western Christians.

At the academic level, the Christian East has often been unfairly dealt with by Western scholars. How many students of history complete their courses of study and cannot recount the major periods in the history of the Byzantine empire? If mention is made of the Orthodox Church in history courses, it is usually pointed out that the Eastern Orthodox Church separated from the Roman Catholic Church in 1054, as the result of a personality conflict between Church leaders. Few Western students are taught to wonder how the oldest Christian Church, the Church of the East, the Church of the original Patriarchates, could have possibly separated from a single Western Patriarchate. They seldom see that the Western Church, after the collapse of the Western part of the Roman empire, moved steadily away from the theological, social, and cultural hegemony of the Christian East, culminating in its departure from the

Eastern Patriarchates in 1054. They fail to understand that it might be far more accurate to speak of the Roman Church as having split from the Eastern Church.

So absurd can the treatment of the Eastern Church become that its witness is wholly distorted, and it becomes the object of the poorest possible scholarly investigation, of scholarship sometimes bordering on persiflage. An outline of Church history popular among fundamentalist Christian scholars perhaps highlights this lack of objectivity. The Eastern Orthodox Church, according to this source, converted the Russian people to Christianity in 988. This is an accurate fact, acknowledging the missionary growth of Orthodox Christianity into Eastern Europe. However, the outline pinpoints 1054 as the year that the Eastern Orthodox Church came into existence, following a rupture of communion between Eastern Christians and the Roman See. Aside from the monumental accomplishment of converting the Russians to Christianity in 988, the Eastern Orthodox Church apparently deserves even greater credit for having done so before coming into existence! In yet another "scholarly" tome, we are told that the Eastern Orthodox Church represents a religious tradition that cannot boast of official recognition before the peace of the Church under St. Constantine, thus compromising its claim to an antiquity that dates before the fourth century. Doubtless it did not occur to the author that formal imperial recognition of the Church was rather difficult to extract from the mouth of a lion.

There are, of course, many exceptions to these unfair and egregiously poor treatments of the Orthodox Church. The famous historian of early Christian monasticism, Professor Derwas Chitty, boldly equated Orthodox Christianity with the Christianity that he discovered in his study of the early Church. Professor Timothy (Kallistos) Ware, now an Orthodox Hierarch, brought his scholarly work at Oxford to the attention of many Westerners, calling them to a remembrance of their lost Eastern heritage. And a host of Orthodox scholars in other European centers of learning, at American institutions like Harvard, Princeton, and Columbia, and elsewhere have been intrepid witnesses to the antiquity of the Orthodox Church. But these scholars constitute an academic elite, possessing the academic élan to put them at the forefront of scholarship. In general, few students or scholars stop to think that the Roman Empire outlived the fifth century, that when Charlemagne spearheaded the *renaissance* of Rome under the Carolingian banner, Rome, to a vast part of the Mediterranean world, had not yet died. Comfortable with their truncated, inaccurate, patently fabricated view of history, Western students and scholars go on in blissful ignorance.

The West, one might indeed observe, has forgotten its past. And when it has spurts of memory, it relegates them to the scholarly realm. It is comfortable with its false past and it perpetuates it in its learning processes. But this comfort is not entirely innocent, nor is the process of relegating the Christian East to the annals of pedantic history unintentional. Much of the memory loss is self-serving, a defense mechanism. This is because, in its ascendancy in the last few centuries, Western society has developed a certain smugness (particularly a religious smugness), to which the East is a living challenge. The East lays claim to an authenticity to which the West cannot. Their complacency challenged, many Westerners respond with a telling enmity for all that is Eastern. Thus it is that a theologian much involved in the ecumenical movement, ironically enough, recently decried the irritant presence of Eastern Orthodoxy in the modern ecclesiastical picture. He bemoaned the fact that one fifth of the world's some billion Christians have survived as a kind of institutional fossil that by all rights, irrelevant as it is to modern Christianity, should not have survived. Claiming to be the genuine Church of the Apostles, with an historical witness

14

matched by no other Christian body, the Eastern Orthodox Church is both a challenge and a threat to modern Christianity, which has been pulled from its roots and which apparently is not anxious to find them, save on its own terms.

Ultimately, the Patristic mind calls the West to a psychology which it has lost, which it knows only in part. The Westerner is scarcely able to grasp this expansive psychology, let alone to acknowledge and correct his own spiritual and intellectual misapprehensions. He finds it difficult to imagine that, as far as the East is from the West, as the Psalmist intones, so far too is Western Christianity from the Christianity of the ancient Church, which, as Mary Chitty once remarked, "the Eastern Orthodox Church of to-day preserves in continuity from the monks of old." It is only by an immense act of will that the Westerner can come to realize that the wisdom of the Orthodox East is not an "alternative" knowledge, not a cognitive system engendered by a strange and foreign culture, but that it is the true light from the East, dawning over "the paradise of God planted toward the East" — an East existing not geographically, but noumenally and ontologically. It is therefore appropriate that we should begin our series on this Patristic wisdom, on the psychology of the Orthodox Fathers, with a volume on humility. For it is only through humility, with a meek spirit, that the West can ever rise to that act of willful submission by which the Patristic mind will be revealed to it.

A certain Persian quoted by Herodotus tearfully remarked, in his now famous adage, that "ἐχθίστη δὲ ὀδύνη ἐστὶ τῶν ἐν ἀνθρώποισι αὕτη, πολλὰ φρονέοντα μηδενὸς κρατέειν." This thought haunts me as I begin this series on the psychology of the Orthodox Fathers. I would, above all else, wish for these few volumes to serve as an introduction to the magnificence of the Orthodox spiritual world. If I should, indeed, aspire to this and yet lack the power to accomplish my end, my lot will be "the bitterest of human sorrow." But I trust that, in a spirit of humility, obedient to the wisdom of the Fathers, repentant for my poor apprehension of the spiritual world so freely given by Grace, and with a faithful love for the truth, I will — with the prayers of my spiritual Father — attain to some success in my endeavor.

1
HUMILITY

THE SPIRITUAL THEORIA *OF HUMILITY*

Tennyson termed humility, "The highest virtue, mother of them all." As unqualified as his praise may be, it pales before that heaped on the virtue of humility by the Orthodox Fathers. Not only did one desert Father call it the greatest of all virtues, but St. Kosmas Aitolos, the great Apostle of modern Greece, calls humility one of the wings, along with love, upon which the Christian soars to Paradise. St. Maximos the Confessor considered it "the first ground of virtues," and St. John Chrysostomos tells us that humility can bear man up on high "from the very abyss of sins." St. Dorotheos of Gaza, warning that "pretentious pride" leads to sure death, commends humility as the path to life itself. St. John Cassian counsels us that, "it is clearly shown that none can attain the end of perfection and purity except through true humility." St. John Climacus, the great theorist of the monastic life, captures the spirit of all of the Orthodox Fathers when he writes that, "However great the life we live may be, we may count it as sterile and false, if we have not acquired a humble heart." At the heart of Orthodox spirituality, indeed at the core of Orthodox theology, is an understanding of humility. All theological thought, all virtues, and all spiritual pursuits collapse like a house built on sand, if they are not rooted in humility.

As exalted and as essential as humility may be in the Western theological tradition, that tradition also pales, as we shall subsequently see, in its understanding of humility, before the insight of the Eastern Fathers. The Blessed Augustine is the source of most Western views of humility and, in fact, most contemporary Protestant theologians, ignoring the witness of the desert, consider Augustine's *humilitas* the source of all but Biblical ideas of the virtue. They especially concentrate on Augustine's belief that humility represents man's awareness of his sin and lowliness before the majesty of God. This awareness represents a static state, a kind of theological state of being, to the Protestant mind. It is for them, moreover, an awareness which God gives to man so that he can understand the absolute depravity of the human condition and the dependence of the human soul on the Grace of God. Especially in Calivinistic theological thought, the Blessed Augustine's concept of humility underlies a denial of humility as an understanding of self, as a product of a personal internal state, and places all emphasis on humility as a revealed gift of Grace. All practical manifestations of this gift, in the forms of self-abasement or acts of humility, are rejected as fictitious.

Most Roman Catholic theological thinkers also base their understanding of humility on the Blessed Augustine. However, they take from his writing not only the idea of humility as a revealed gift of Grace, but also acknowledge Augustine's deeper understanding of humility as a product of self-knowledge. They see the potential for humility in man's actions, as well as his reception of Divine Grace. Humility becomes a far more human trait, that can be translated into human action through self-abasement and service. In the first case, one accomplishes humility through *obedience to superiors,* through a conscious understanding of one's lowliness before the greater worth of others, and through a thorough awareness of one's proclivity toward the sinful. In the second case, the human being comes to express his sense of lowliness through *service to others,* which constitutes a kind of external manifestation of a mentalistic understanding of humility, an imitation, in essence, of the submission of Christ to the Will of the Father.

Both the Protestant and the Roman Catholic theological concepts of humility have deeply affected the popular view of that virtue in contemporary Western society. The Protestant concept, when stripped of its theological structure and meaning, reduces to a humanistic statement of humility that is both popular and timely. Humility, according to the humanistic thinker, has its source in the natural goodness of man, in his innate ability to combat evil, in man's resilient capacity for retrieving himself from the abyss of moral wrong. Humility accrues to the individual and is an exercise of his higher nature. It expresses the highest human traits. It is given to man, not by God's Grace in recognition of sinful human nature, as in Protestant thought, but is bequeathed to him by "Nature," by virtue of the lofty *human* heights to which he is called. And all of this can, in an uglier form of expression, give forth the most mundane view of humility: a trait which characterizes those who respect and uphold others as much as themselves.

The Roman Catholic idea of humility, when secularized and separated from its theological base, provides us with the modern vision of self-sacrifice, of simple altruism. According to this equally prevalent view of humility, a human exalts his own self-worth by an understanding of his need for others, for the "human family." Because an understanding of one's need for others results only from self-knowledge and introspection, this secularized view of humility takes on a pseudo-spiritual dimension. But such a form of humility is, in fact, wholly at odds with the *humilitas* of the Blessed Augustine, from which the Roman Catholic idea of the virtue is drawn. Whereas Augustine predicated altruism and self-sacrifice on ultimate self-abasement, the secularized version of his formulation begins with no such insight; rather, as we have indicated, self-worth and self-esteem are the basic elements toward which humble service to others is directed. The internal awareness of one's lowliness before others is wholly absent in this formulation. Indeed, so rife and so overpowering is this secular statement of the traditional view of the Latin spiritualists, that it has contaminated, as we shall eventually argue, the very nature of its practical expression in Western monasticism.

The Eastern Fathers envision humility with far greater profundity and complexity. Neither are they limited, as in the West, by an indebtedness to one or two Fathers or Doctors of the Church for their basic precepts, nor does their understanding of humility flow forth from Biblical exegesis and hermeneutic pursuits separated from the witness of experience. The Eastern Fathers understand humility as an effusive virtue found in Scripture, in the Fathers of the desert, dwelling in the nature of God and man, and as imminent as their own spiritual lives. Their understanding neither contradicts nor supersedes the notions of humility found in Protestant and Roman Catholic thought — indeed, in contemporary humanistic thought. More correctly, the Eastern Fathers bring these elements into proper perspective, defining and delimiting their worth and their roles in the authentic acquisition of humility. Orthodox theological thinkers do not limit humility, as in the Protestant tradition, to a mere spiritual characteristic, devoid of relationship to the human spirit. At the same time, they do not conceive of humility in so drastically a human way as traditional Roman Catholic thinkers, who overemphasize, from an Eastern perspective, conscious self-abasement and service.

For the Orthodox Christian, humility begins in the " ἄκρα ταπείνωσις ," or extreme humility, of Christ, who, as God, deigned to take the form of a man and sacrifice Himself for the sake of all men. It is in the condescension of God, becoming intimately bound to his own creation, that the Orthodox Fathers have always found the source of humility. It is in the nature of God Himself that humility dwells. And this characteristic of God, simply because it belongs to a God Who is transcendent, unknowable in essence, and beyond human comprehension, is not a simple "quality" or adornment, as we attribute such to a human. It is a power of a metaphysical kind, one of the attributes of God, and therefore of ontological significance. It relates to a real power, a literal force that, like God, touches on all mankind. It is inherent, indeed, in the Redeeming Sacrifice of Christ. To aspire to humility is, for the Orthodox Christian, to participate in an energy emanating from God, to join oneself to a living aspect of God, actually to participate in divinity itself. Imitation and mere self-knowledge are inadequate in bringing the human to such an understanding and experience of humility.

If humility belongs to the nature of God and signifies the redemptive work of Christ, it also dwells within man as a touchstone of his divine potential. In Orthodox theology, salvation is nothing less than the enlightenment of man (a bold statement supported by the no less candid words of St. Nikodemos of the Holy Mountain: "Without enlightenment, there is no salvation"). It is man's awareness of the divinity that dwells within him, his union by Grace with God (even to some extent in the present life), his *theosis*, or divinization. To attain salvation, in the eyes of the Eastern Fathers, is to become divine, to be "participants in the divine nature" [" γένησθε θείας κοινωνοί φύσεως "] (II Peter 1:4); for, as St. Gregory Nazianzen has amazingly stated, God, for the sake of man, took human form, that men might become gods. This union with God through Grace, the salvation of man by his direct and close participation in God's energies, is expressly tied to the idea of humility.

Humility, St. John Chrysostomos tells us, is proper to the divine potential within man, the light of Christ which burns in the human heart, just as pride is appropriate to the fallen man. It was through pride, an inner desire to usurp the divinity of God, that the Evil One, Lucifer, fell from his participation in divinity. This pride, with its source in the Prince of Darkness, is the quality, the very force, which separates man from his participation in God, the great power of the human ego which clouds the image of God within man. Because he thinks of himself as a creator (and thus generates for himself the whole world of passion and lust), because he elevates himself above the Creator and imagines that what he can comprehend with his mind constitutes all that there is, man has distorted his rightful relationship to God. And this distortion is empowered by pride, perpetuated by this real, driving, metaphysical force. Pride is the veritable source of man's damnation, of his separation from his own divinity within God. And humility is the real, driving, metaphysical force by which man can recapture his divine image, indeed find salvation.

Humility is within human grasp when a person touches, first, the humility of God, when he fully realizes, and responds to, the extreme humility of the Redemptive Sacrifice of Christ. Humility originates in the proper understanding and experience of God. Once a person can comprehend divine humility, he is propelled, as it were, toward self-understanding, toward discovering, through this aspect of God, more of the God Who indwells him. He is turned within, towards the inner life, where he comes to behold his own divine potential. Self-knowledge is, in effect, simply part of a process: the process of discovering, through the witness of His humble assumption of human form, God's presence within man. It is the vision of God in this way, the realization of his close presence in the human, that produces humility — a humility drawn from a proper understanding of God, spawned by self-knowledge, and ultimately vivified by the humility that emanates from God Himself. Neither is humility an adornment of man, nor is it simply an attribute of self-knowledge. To the Eastern Fathers, humility is that great awe that the fallen race of men has before the image of God lying deep within, an awe which is part of the energies of God.

THE PSYCHOLOGICAL PRAXIS OF HUMILITY

Our theological consideration of humility has emphasized that, from the standpoint of an Orthodox cosmology, humility is not a simple concept. It is not just an adornment of the personality, a human trait, but it proceeds from an understanding of both God and man. Because of this, we cannot speak of a humble man simply as one who incorporates into his ethical system a certain sense of the worth of others, balanced against a fair and unexaggerated sense of his own personal worth. Humility cannot be, moreover, a style of self-presentation, in which one fancies the humble person to be one who "listens well" and does not impose his own values and perspectives on others. Nor can one ultimately think of humility as a "personal" virtue, as something that rises from the person alone. None of these images of humility captures the Orthodox Patristic understanding of the concept, for again the psychology of the Fathers never separates the mind from the spirit, the person from interaction with God. An Orthodox concept of humility emerges only when theological theory comes into actual practice, when the spiritual force of humility is expressed through the perceptive Christian.

True humility, we might argue, has little to do with behaviors alone; rather, it reaches into the very core of man's identity, into that realm where the divine potential and human fallibility and corruption come into confrontation. It is produced by an essentially spiritual or theological revelation, in that realm, of the great chasm that separates the fallen man from the image of God that dwells within him. As one beholds the perfection and moral highness to which the human is called (and to which, to some extent, he is naturally inclined), he is at once struck by the disparity between this perfection and the actual state of his life. He looks upon his behaviors and accomplishments, and somehow they wax faint before the inner example of perfection epitomized externally in the life of Christ. And this sense, this understanding of the contrast between what one is and what one is called to be, is what humility is. It cannot take place without the spiritual revelation of the potential for perfection to which every Christian is called, and it cannot take meaning without the mind's reflection on the failure of man and the world to realize that potential.

The first practice of humility, then, is a passive one, which does not necessarily relate to behaviors. It involves the internal world, the mental world, indeed a special world where the spirit and mind meet, where theological insight is transformed into self-understanding and self-evaluation. Here one must muster all of his objective understanding and grasp the relationship between God and man, understand the Fall and the *novus homo,* the man renewed by Christ's redemptive powers, by detachment from all ideas of self-worth, from all attachments to the sensuous world. A human being in this realm must boldly offer up his own life against the perfection of God and with total acceptance suffer the inevitable, understandable "humiliation" by which even the best in human life is shattered and mocked. In this contrast between the divine potential and human reality, we have already said, humility is born. But even more importantly, a process of self-abasement begins, by which the person spurns his own mind, his own will, and aspires to attain the mind of God, the mind of the Fathers, that mind which is in Christ [" τοῦτο γὰρ φρονείσθω ἐν ὑμῖν ὃ καὶ ἐν Χριστῷ "] (Philippians 2:5).

A man who practices self-abasement, who pursues the Will of God, evidences, of course, this practice in his external behaviors. Certainly he will defer to the thoughts of others, since neither his human thoughts nor those of others are of prime interest to him. Thus it is that we see many of the desert Fathers practicing a humility in which, even though they may be correct in their own statements and another may be technically wrong, they find no motivation in themselves to proffer their own correct views or to expose the falsity of those of another. The focus of such a spiritual man's life is toward perfection, not the relative correctness of human thought. Such a man may also show ostensibly super-human patience and the ability to endure the derision of others to a point unattainable by most. He may seem to be, in the apt, if ugly, metaphor for humility, a "doormat," upon whom everyone treads. His behaviors may, indeed, appear to be those of the humble man as we commonly imagine him, seemingly separated, therefore, from the humble man whom we have characterized as a product of a unique, internal, spiritual sense of humility.

And here is the crux in understanding true humility, spiritual humility, the humility that originates in inner processes, the humility that issues forth from the psychology of the Fathers. It is not a humility that can be understood from merely observing behaviors. External signs of humility (an apparent deference to the will of others, for example) are not always symptomatic of spiritual humility. They are often actually human traits, controlled, begotten, and observed by the individual mind. They can be deliberate and contrived behaviors. True humility, on the other hand, must derive from something internal, from a personal disposition prompted by the spiritual revelation of the chasm between man's fallen state and his divine potential, to which we have referred. Such a sense, such a way of approaching the world, combines the force of the spirit and the mind and, thus, the behaviors emitted by such spiritually aware people are neither deliberate nor contrived. In fact, one might say that the truly humble man cannot indeed know that he is humble. His humility does not come from his mind or from some aspect of his personality; it has its source in divine revelation. While the man who behaves

25

in a humble way as a result of an internal spiritual state cannot behold his behaviors, one who shows common humility is able not only to observe his behaviors, but to control them. From one, humility proceeds out of the soul; from the other, humility flows forth from the mind.

Let us understand, therefore, that humility must always be approached with caution. Just as it is almost impossible to understand the internal world of another, so it is extremely difficult to understand true humility from nothing more than an observation of external behaviors. We have said that one may have humble traits without, in fact, there existing the inner state by which true humility is born. At the same time, there have been Fathers who attained to an understanding of humility internally, but never demonstrated to any great extent the external signs which we might associate with popular views of humility. Here, of course, all observed behavior becomes second-ary, since it gives us little indication of the internal life of the spiritual man. As puzzling as this circumstance may seem at first sight, it is actually quite simple to understand. The Fathers who attained to this state call us, by their singular and God-ordained witness, to a higher understanding of humility, giving us striking evidence that mere behaviors do not signal the presence of humility. Their humility lay in their special accomplishment of a humility above humility, revealed, in most circumstances, only after their deaths. Eschewing even the possibility of praise for their humility, they lift the interaction of mind and spirit into a realm where even their personal psychology seems somehow spiritual.

Because the psychology of the Fathers captures humility as a passive thing, it exposes the common view of humility as a form of pride, as a false humility, as "pride that apes humility," in the words of Coleridge. It exposes the world of behaviors, the world of acting, the world of spiritual theatre. The blending of spiritual insight with a certain external meekness both authenticates true humility and betrays false humility. True humility proceeds from the truth of the spirit; false humility is the product of the person alone. Thus the Orthodox view of humility allows us to look deeply into the many pitfalls in spiritual life, into the many opportunities for a disjointed spiritual life. We can look so much more profoundly on the nature of spirituality as it surrounds us and unmask it, when it is false, so as to free ourselves for true spiritual pursuits. We are allowed a practical understanding of humility that is both instructive and inspiring. Let us, then, look at a number of examples of spiritual life today and discover within them the operation of false humility and thereby benefit from the insight given to us by the Fathers and their deep, authentic notion of humility. Just as the anecdotes from the desert Fathers translated and set forth in chapter three tell us something of humility by genuine examples of what it is, let our following comments serve to teach us something of humility by studying what it is not. To see true humility can inspire us. To understand false humility can protect us.

Monasticism and Spiritual Deception. Perhaps nowhere, as in monasticism, can one come to understand the meaning of humility. The way of life to which the monastic is called is one primarily of developing the spiritual self, of conforming the worldly self, the fallen man, to the spiritual image hidden within. It is a way in which the mind and the spirit are brought closer together, so that the individual will dies to the Will of God and the fallen nature succumbs to the inviting nostalgia of the soul for its higher state. The monastic life, in effect, brings the contrast between man's divinity and his humanity into an acute focus, thus almost automatically producing humility. And this true humility not only serves the person engaged in the monastic struggle, but it presents to others a living example, to the extent that a monk succeeds in his task, of the higher nature of man. The monk comes to personify the internal life, to give it actual human form.

Any authentic practitioner of monasticism lives that life as a philosophical life, as a life of struggle between the fallen and the exalted, as a life which portrays principles, inner values, and theology itself. It is a life of mind and spirit working in synergy toward perfection.

Western monasticism, in accordance with the course of Western intellectual and religious thought, has come to separate the spiritual and mentalistic lives of the monastic. Terms like humility and obedience come to have wholly exterior meaning, expressed in legalistic nomenclature. The monastic takes "vows" by which he dedicates himself, by an act of the will, to avoidance of the worldly life, to concentration on the spiritual, to the devotion of his life to service to others. And he does this by acquiring humble traits, learning always to put another before himself and to follow precisely the orders of his superiors. But this is not monasticism, nor is this kind of humility genuine. An Eastern monk, though he must have the same resolve to pursue the non-worldly, does not end his spiritual ascent at that point. Having resolved to obey and think first of others, to concentrate on the spiritual life, and to break his will, he encounters the spiritual self. And once encountering that self, once beholding the perfection to which the Divine Will beckons, he sees the great distance between himself and his divine potential. From this he develops inner humility, which naturally disposes him toward service to others and self-abasement. And herein lies the great, inestimable difference between the true humility of Eastern monasticism and the false humility which has developed in the modern West. The former is an inner state that acts on the mind; the latter is a human trait imposed by the mind on action and on external behaviors.

I would be remiss, were I to treat only with Western monasticism as such. There is also, though in an infant stage of development, a growing Orthodox monasticism in the West. There are a few monastic institutions which, by virtue of having been "transplanted," as it were, to the West (after the Communist persecutions of Orthodox Eastern Europe), preserve an ancient monasticism. Others have drawn from the strength of these monasteries and have founded healthy, thriving, indigenous monasteries. But a growing number of patently bogus monastics, insufficiently sober in their understanding of Orthodoxy, have begun to create a "modernized" monasticism, which conforms itself to the religious consciousness of the West. At times, this has become absurd, with monasteries proposing that total fabrications of religious rules (more often than not adaptations of Western monastic life) are somehow consistent with the existence of various *typika*, by which Eastern Orthodox monasteries determine for themselves certain *very minor* variances in rubrics and practice. But at the core of this "renovationist" monasticism is, in fact, a self-ordained, self-created sense of monasticism. This leads one directly to a wholly Western view of self, of service, and ultimately of humility. Correspondingly, it leads one away from the true spirit that is naturally produced by a traditional, inner monasticism, in which true humility is revealed. Since this renovationist monasticism is created by self-reliance and the mind, it produces a false humility.

As though this terrible flaw were not sufficiently serious, a number of Orthodox monastics in the West have begun to react to renovationist monasticism by a "perfect monasticism," in which absolutely every element of classical Orthodox monasticism is assiduously studied and employed. A wrong note in singing one of the ancient tones during services is thought to be a sign of disrespect for tradition, an arrogance reminiscent of those who write their own services. The minor differences allowed by the *typika* between practices in various monasteries suddenly become issues of "right" and "wrong" practice, or fabrication and innovation. The canons of the Church, the rudder by which the spiritual ship is guided, become separated from their utility and are transformed into veritable cannons. Firing legalistic accusations at one another, these monastics simply devastate and sink, not only their enemies, but, by violating basic Christian charity, themselves. And all of this is done in the name of what one Old Calendar Greek Bishop, Cyprian of Oropos and Fili, has called "super-correctness," a kind of attainment to external perfection in the techniques of monasticism, as it were, which presents itself to the deluded monastic as a humility born of hyperbolic respect for the Church.

In fact, this apparent humility is nothing but a form of false humility, a *perceived* humility, based on a purely mental assessment of things spiritual. And since it is only mental, those who practice it are not free from the deception, misrepresentation, and vanity that accompany all things of the fallen mind. Thus we see that these poor monastics, so accomplished in all that is external, begin to lose control of basic internal processes. They move from ecclesiastical and theological condemnations of those who do not meet their standards of external spiritual purity to actual personal attacks. So it is that I recently heard of a monastic, perceived by some very accomplished monks to be a threat, apparently, to their peculiar view of the spiritual life, being characterized as mentally ill and untrustworthy. In another egregious case of calumny, a widowed monk was once described as a man who had been involved in a marriage that "did not work out." Again a certain religious from a Greek and aristocratic Spanish background came under the attack of a group of monks who questioned his ancestry and relegated him to an ethnic group which, in their lamentably curious, if not racist, view, apparently placed him in a negative light. In another case, a very renowned Orthodox Abbess, a former princess, was accused of misrepresenting herself as a member of the royalty. Often only vaguely familiar with those whom they attack,

30

moreover, these falsely humble monks will claim the most intimate and complete familiarity with their adversaries. Christian charity, in effect, gives forth to the natural, fallen human urge to gossip and slander others — especially those who are perceived as threatening. And blinded by false humility, such monks are tragically unaware that their sight has been taken from them.

The greater tragedy of this "super-correct" monasticism is often overlooked by all of us. On the one hand, it leads those in society, looking on the monastic life as a standard of spiritual behavior, to despair about the reality of the Christian virtues. Not understanding the complex nature of those virtues and the occasion for spiritual deception, they are tempted to think that monasticism is a false path toward perfection, seeing so little compassion, love, and charity in monks who live the most exemplary monastic life from the standpoint of externality. Or, if they are deeply religious and overlook these flaws, they can themselves begin to emulate these deluded monks, at first maybe benefiting from their inevitable spiritual sobriety, but later perhaps succumbing to the less savory example of calumny and slander. On the other hand, there are those who themselves rather self-righteously condemn these deluded monastics as having accomplished nothing. This, too, is a danger, since, were it not for the high quality of their efforts in the spiritual life, these monks would never have risen to the point that something so subtle as false humility could befall them. In both instances, one must strive to elevate the mind to a spiritual understanding of humility and overcome the merely mentalistic notion of that virtue.

Pride Masquerades as Humility. There is also a strange pride which presents itself as the standard of humility. This false humility is almost wholly the product of self-righteous hypocrisy. It is perhaps, indeed, the most transparent kind of false humility — and yet, it is probably the most frequent. I saw it in its most spontaneous form once while visiting the city of San Francisco. In this, the most Orthodox of American cities (the city where St. Peter the Aleut was martyred by Jesuits in the nineteenth century and where the relics of a contemporary saint, Blessed Archbishop John Maximovitch, rest), I felt less out of place as an Orthodox clergyman among predominantly non-Orthodox people. Given this, I was astounded when a passer-by commented, within my hearing, that I was "nothing more than a Pharisee." It surprised me, too, that his companion responded with rather unflattering remarks about my appearance. While this is not an unusual occurence among Orthodox clergymen who keep traditional dress, I had been particularly struck because it had happened in a place where I did not expect it. And this prompted me to think more seriously about these hecklers.

Many find, in their desire to "fit into society," a rather strange basis upon which to accuse others of arrogance. Walking down the street in the traditional garb of an Orthodox clergyman almost immediately puts one out of step with the rest of society. And it is precisely this that identifies a Christian. If anything could be said about the Pharisees, aside from their spiritual pride, it would be that they were, indeed, in the mainstream of the then contemporary religious scene. And it was, to be sure, not their manner of dress which brought Christ's condemnation upon them. It was precisely their acceptance in society, their exploitation of religion as a way of gaining social respect. And above that, their judgmentalism and wholly external grasp of the spiritual were the very things which the Christian message so fundamentally challenged. If there were modern Pharisees, it would seem to me that one might find them on the street, condemning Priests in clerical garb as Pharisaical, all the while imagining themselves humble by adhering to the social trend.

We see this same false humility in the sometimes

32

fanatic avoidance of the special dress, beard, and hair prescribed for Orthodox clergymen in the 102 canons of the Sixth Ecumenical Council. Especially in the United States, Orthodox clergymen have proclaimed that they must not separate themselves from the laity by their dress. They eschew the traditional form of dress with such great vehemence that a modernist clergyman once told me that he would commit suicide before he would appear on the street in Orthodox clerical clothing. It is the vehemence of these declarations which betrays the ostensible humility of not wishing to separate oneself from the laity. (In fact, of course, the laity themselves, in traditional Orthodoxy, are also required to separate themselves from the prevailing fashions of the times.) Amidst the historically untenable protestation that Orthodox clerical dress derives from the "Turks," that it is Pharisaical, or that it is simply uncomfortable, one discerns that the actual problem is that the clergy lack two forms of humility: one which would prompt them to respect the Church canons (with which they take constant exception); another which would allow them to walk the streets witnessing their Faith to the heterodox, standing as reminders of the spiritual in a wholly materialistic world, and accepting the inevitable ridicule of those who wish to be rude. They do not, in fact, follow the modern dress trend out of humility, but out of a fear of humiliation! Theirs is a clear example of false humility.

This false humility in some Orthodox clergy is not limited to external dress. Often it manifests itself in a deep internal misunderstanding of Church tradition and of the role of the clergy in the Church. Actually from the very Early Church, Orthodox lay people have continued the habit of kissing a cleric's hand as a sign of respect for his religious role. Many contemporary Orthodox clergymen spurn this practice, pointing out that, as with traditional clerical dress, it elevates the Priest above the people. In truth, the practice has traditionally been accepted in the

Church as a means by which the people can express their humility before the holy, the image of which is embodied in the Priest. When a Priest's hand is kissed, the kiss acknowledges the fact that he touches the Holy Eucharist, which elevates not the man, but the holiness with which he interacts in a literal way. As well, other religious in the Church, such as the Abbess of a monastery or a particularly holy elder or spiritual advisor without priestly orders, are afforded this honor by virtue of the fact that their lives are elevated and touch on the holy.

A cleric who disdains the practice of hand kissing often shows, by his apparent claim to humility, a certain hidden arrogance. False humility is that humility which is contrived and controlled by the human will. The desire to demonstrate to others that one is unworthy of respect, therefore, is actually an occasion for taking pride in the appearance of humility. And that pride lurks in such a cleric is easily demonstrated. Those who disdain this practice because it elevates them misapprehend, in the first place, the fact that the kiss is meant to rise up to the holy, not the individual himself. It is by this same logic that kissing an Icon, for example, is not idolatrous. The Priest must set himself aside, when he understands his religious role, and become a mere image. That he thinks the kiss is directed toward him means that he has usurped the honor due his rank and the Grace operating within him, somehow fancying himself more than a Priestly Icon. He denies, therefore, the lay people a vehicle for expressing their own humility before the holy. If such clerics were not, indeed, falsely humble, they would not imagine themselves the objects of respect when their hands are kissed, but, like my own spiritual Father, who tells me that he feels as though he is under the feet of those who kiss his hand, would show true humility.

Another rather disturbing and dangerous example of pride masquerading as humility has simply devastated the Orthodox Church in this century. It comes to us in the form of ecumenism. The Eastern Orthodox Church, with historical foundations for the claim, has always maintained that it continues the very Church of the Apostles, the Church established on earth by Christ Himself. Our Fathers, throughout the centuries, have taken seriously the burden of preserving the pristine truth of early Christianity. They have practiced a conscious conservativism, avoiding trendy involvement in the spirit of any particular age, lest they tarnish with temporal thinking the eternal witness passed down to them from the Apostles. In this process of preserving an eternal truth from the vicissitudes of various ages, they have used conservativism as a tool, and they have always, if one reads their words with care, avoided an arrogant view of their role, even when they were called to severe positions in protecting the traditions of the Church. They always felt it their first purpose to proclaim the absolute historical and spiritual primacy of the Orthodox Church in a humble way, preserving the Church as the final resort of those who might stray away, over the centuries, from her authentic witness. In effect, the Orthodox Church is the mother of true ecumenism. It has been Her role to preserve the true message of Christ in its purest form, offering it up to the whole world as the standard and banner of truth.

Many contemporary Orthodox clergymen and lay people have come to think that the Orthodox Church's claim to primacy is an arrogant one which is an impediment to the spread of the Christian message. They often hold up the example of would-be traditionalist Orthodox, who imagine their Orthodoxy to be some exclusive right belonging to them alone and who almost happily condemn all others as heretics. They quite rightly point out that such "tradition" has its source in personal pride and violates the missionary conscience of the true Christian. One might even agree with them, were they to say that such "traditionalists" suffer from deep, hidden pride. One cannot, however, countenance the conclusion that, because errant traditionalists violate the Christian spirit, their understanding of the primacy of Orthodoxy must be put aside. This is in itself a form of false humility, for when we proclaim the primacy of Orthodoxy, if it is not a personal possession or a personal understanding, we do so without violating our own personal humility.

One can find a personal witness to divine primacy arrogant only if he imagines that divine primacy to be a personal belief and not, as it is, a divine revelation. In fact, there is perhaps no greater sign of humility than that of dedicating oneself to a truth which is absolute, which transcends the person and personal opinion, of boasting, as it were, of that which is above the individual. It is precisely this humility which St. Paul reveals to us when, boasting of his sufferings and exploits, he tells us that they have meaning only in Jesus Christ. One cannot so boast if he thinks that Orthodoxy rises out of him, not out of God. Such a thought is horribly prideful and those who think thus, proclaiming that out of humility they cannot proclaim their religion to be the true religion, arrogantly deny Orthodox tradition, sadly deny a strong witness to others, and betray themselves as falsely humble. Such ecumenism is not really a form of humble love for others and for their Faith; it is a denial of the Orthodox Faith. It stands nakedly inadequate before the true ecumenism of the Fathers.

False Humility and the Imitation of the Holy. In his *De Imitatione Christi,* the great Western spiritualist, Thomas à Kempis, popularized the idea of holiness as an imitation of the life of Christ. His theory and the theories and practices which grew out of his observations are based on the idea that if one imitates Christ and the Saints, his practice will elevate him to the stature of those whom he imitates. If one consciously patterns his life, both in actions and in thoughts, after the life of Christ or the lives of the Saints, he will ultimately share both in the nature and the quality of their lives. Imitation, in short, can be practiced as a means to the end of spiritual transformation. Western monasticism has, as we have previously argued, been heavily influenced by these kinds of mentalistic spiritualities, in which the conscious control of behaviors and attitudes constitutes, to some extent, the whole of the spiritual life. Higher spirituality flows simply from these practices, and humility is ultimately wrought by one's abandonment of personal psychology for the psychology of another. This psychogenic process presumably leads to a mystical imitation of Christ Himself, the individual humbly putting himself aside, that Christ might dwell within him. And it is a dangerously compelling view of the spiritual life.

The Eastern Fathers, however, would find the imitation of the Saints and Christ, as put forth in Western spirituality, frightfully naive. Moreover, they would consider the humility involved in that spirituality a false humility. Firstly, it is impossible for the human being to put aside his own ego, his own life, simply by imitating someone holy. The logical consequence of such imitation is spiritual pride. If one puts himself aside in order to identify with someone who is presented to him as a master of spiritual accomplishment, he inevitably runs the risk of thinking that, by imitating such a person, he too can achieve to the spiritual fame attached to that person. And if one imitates Christ under the guise of putting aside his own self, he has accomplished the dubiously humble goal of uniting himself with the Son of God by an act of will — by an imitative process. Union with Christ, however, as the Eastern Fathers have always taught and as Christian doctrine avers, is a gift of Grace, not the result of something like imitation. While our works and ascetic practices can lift us up to the realm of God's Grace, participation in the divine is wholly separate from those efforts as such. In such a context, the mere idea of imitation as a sufficient means to spiritual transformation seems ludicrous.

Secondly, when we are called to view ourselves vis-à-vis Christ, the Saints, or the Fathers of the Church, it is in a spirit of emulation, not imitation. The ideas of emulation and, to some extent, obedience are implicit in St. Paul's injunction that the Christian be an imitator of Christ. The Greek sense of imitation, not withstanding the derivation of the word "mimic" from the Greek, implies an adherence to a model, not mimicry. Thus, the Fathers are set before us as *standards to which we should strive,* but whom we could not hope to imitate. Anyone who has read early Patristic texts on spiritual development is struck by the fact that the very earliest spiritual writers, who for us are giants of ascetic and spiritualistic attainment, thought themselves unworthy of the Fathers before them. There has been, from the very beginning of Christianity, an emphasis on the unattainable stature of the ancients. Always our Fathers have been presented as the highest standards, who, when we measure ourselves against them, humble us because of the highness of their virtues. The humility that we find in this process, then, has nothing to do with the humility of self-abandonment. It is a far more intricate kind of humility. It is a humility which teaches us how lowly we are, how far we are from spiritual attainment, and how untouchable the great spiritual giants of our Church actually are. With this humility, we never reckon ourselves to be worthy of participation in the divine. And it is only, of course, in such real humility, in such a profound sense of unworthiness, that our desire to emulate the Fathers is ever rewarded by true union with, and participation in, the divine.

At another level, it is folly for us to imitate the Fathers. They were divinely ordained by God to be the standards of Christian perfection, against which we might ourselves perfect humility. In this age of spiritual delusion, many look upon the words of the Fathers, who speak of lust, greed, envy, and human weaknesses known to all of us, thinking that the Fathers are speaking of our own lowly traits. When the desert Fathers speak of lust, however, they refer to a force within the human which does battle with the flesh, which resists its transformation by contact with the divine. The filth, degeneracy, and prurient deformities of the mind and body that are today called lust are unknown to these angels in the flesh. Their greed is that of men who left all things of the world, hardly to be compared to the horrible, frenzied materialism that reigns in our day. Their envy is the envy of the innocent, not the vicious jealousy of the self-centered modern men. Their human weaknesses are, by comparison to our own, the weaknesses of the saintly. So it is that spiritual guides tell us that in fact we should *not* consciously ape the actions of these spiritual masters. If we do, we will attain nothing, even if we perfectly mock their actions. For we will have missed their true purpose: that of creating within us the humility which comes from knowing their unattainable height and our miserable lowliness. By imitating them and thinking that we equal them, we succumb to pride. By emulating them and failing to equal them, we attain to true humility.

The Consequences of False Humility and Spiritual Deception. As we have observed, false humility grows out of a separation of the mind from the spirit. An individual suffering from this spiritual affliction is able to cover his proud thoughts with an external appearance of humility. This accomplishment is not unlike that of an actor, who, by manipulating his observers and deliberately controlling his self-presentation, can deceive others into thinking that he is humble. And he takes from this a certain unseemly pleasure; *i.e.*, the comfort of knowing that his true pride has been hidden. His humility belongs entirely to the mind. The truly humble person, however, derives his humility, we have argued, from an inner revelation of his estrangement from the perfection to which the light of God within man naturally calls him. This revelation, in an effulgence of repentance, casts its light upon the whole person, and the mind instinctively and naturally operates in a spiritual way. The fallen humanity within us becomes spontaneously humble before the majesty of the divine potential. The falsely humble man, therefore, is quite easily understood, if one carefully analyzes his spiritual life; for his behaviors and mind will ultimately lack this connection with his religious life. There will be a disparity between what he does and what he advocates, what he "practices" and what he "preaches." Living to deceive others, though never actually deceiving himself, he finally betrays himself even to those whom he would deceive.

There is, however, a deeper spiritual deception which can result from unchecked false humility. This frightful, unbelievably complex state is called, by the Greek Fathers, πλάνη [plane]. If a falsely humble person pursues his course in deceiving others and his deceit is not discovered, he falls into this terrible condition. Prompted by the praise of others, subject to demonic forces which further blind his objectivity, he comes to think that he is actually humble, deceiving not only the observer, but himself. The pleasure taken from false humility and the praise of others is no longer that of having hidden some inner pride, of having protected the ego; rather, it is now a false spiritual pleasure, a misguided notion that mentally contrived, external behaviors are, in fact, the products of an inner spiritual force. In a mockery of true spiritual life, such victims of spiritual delusion come to imagine that they have found the bridge between the mind and the spirit which characterizes true humility. They begin to see in their experiences the experiences of the enlightened spiritual Fathers. In an exact, but deceptive, duplication of the spiritual process by which humility is born, these poor souls behold a contrast deep within themselves that suggests that they have acquired humility by divine revelation.

In fact, the contrast which these individuals find within themselves is not an acknowledgement of the chasm which exists between their divine potential, which is God dwelling within man, and their own human imperfection. What they behold is the chasm between what they are as imperfect humans and what they can personally become. It is not a contrast between our fallen selves and the image of God in man, which humbles us because of the tarnish with which we have encrusted this image by our sins, but a contrast between false humility and the potential for authenticating that humility by some pristine inner self. This is not an easy thing to understand, nor is it surprising that those who fall to *plane* are unaware that they have not touched something spiritual within them, but that they are still within the realm of personal psychology. They imagine that they can attain the perfect image of themselves which they have only *apparently* beheld spiritually. In so doing, their external humble acts take on a spiritual dimension. They no longer seem deceptive. The truly humble man, on the other hand, beholds a majesty within himself that he feels he can never achieve — nor can he; for ultimate perfection in Christ is wrought by Grace. If the truly humble man's external behaviors become humble, he never imagines that these come forth, by God's Grace, through spiritual revelation. He is unaware of his humility.

The man who is falsely humble is an anguished man, since his supposed inner spirituality is a sham, without Grace, without that force by which his personality might be transformed. His inner revelation is in actuality the core of the personality, the unformed energy of the ego. It is pure pride, the same pride which sits at the foundations of man's fall. It reveals itself, in a pseudospiritual, essentially psychological way, as a deep inner sense, telling the individual that at his very core he is perfect, good, and endowed with the attributes of God. It is that same whisper which Satan heard and which he has perpetuated in the human race. It tells the falsely humble man that somewhere within, beyond his personality and his external deceptiveness, he is perfect, special, if not superior and among the elect. And the naive human, tainted with sin, imagines that this whisper is what the Fathers mean by the image of God within man, by the true inner man.

Thinking himself perfect at a deep, personal level, the spiritually deluded man tends to overlook his own psychology, excusing it on the basis of the deeper life to which he is supposedly called. And in this departure from careful self-control, he loses control of his own psychology and becomes the victim of forces which he cannot even begin to recognize. The most vitriolic, horrendous motivations he can ignore, thinking that he is turning his attention to the spiritual center within him. He comes to violate Christian charity and compassion, under the external guise of humility, at times even extolling the virtues of true humility and condemning those whom he finds to be falsely humble. If he is a clergyman, he finds fault with other clergymen. If he is a layman, he finds fault with all those around him and with his spiritual leaders. He suddenly finds himself the guardian of all that is true, imagining that all others are deluded. And so encompassing is this need to justify his own perfection, that he becomes a champion of slander, attributing to others every possible sin, even if he must lie to do so. And here begins his anguish.

Since the man suffering from false pride is not truly enlightened from within, but from the depths of his mind, he cannot ultimately understand himself. One enlightened by the spirit can achieve such detachment from himself that he can observe his own motivations objectively — indeed, the *mind*, as St. Gregory Palamas astoundingly writes, can turn and look upon itself.

Without this spiritual power, a man is the victim of his own mental world. Lurking in the subliminal levels of the mind of the spiritually deluded man, then, is an awareness of his deceptive behaviors, indeed a knowledge that he has falsely accused others and only pretends, in his external behaviors, to be humble and holy. When this comes to him, he suffers the anguish of his conscience and he stands always at the threshold of spiritual death or spiritual life. If he turns to the dark side, he blots out the record of his conscience, saying that he is acting as he does for the good estate of the Church. Perhaps he will even come to think that his self-doubt (actually guilt) is itself a sign of humility. If he is a religious, he fancies himself a great champion of spirituality. If he is a lay person, he often stands amazed at the depth of his spiritual accomplishment and elevates himself above the religious. If, however, he succumbs to the light of his conscience, he enters into the deepest repentance and begins anew his search for the true spiritual life. In the one instance, serving false spirituality, he continues his course of action with revenge and hatred for all who expose his spiritual delusion. He justifies himself by recalling that perfection which he has so uniquely (albeit falsely) found within him. In the second instance, the deluded man, by the mercy of God, understands that it is he who stands with all guilt. And his anguish leads him to the True God, to true humility.

Every monastic, every spiritual aspirant (and this almost without exception), is tempted by false humility. This is only natural, since each of us has not only the image of God within, but has pride sitting upon the throne of the ego. Confession, obedience, and the denial of self-will (all things which, to the spiritually deluded man, while he advocates them for others, are accursed to him personally) can cure us of our egotistical self-centeredness. And, as we have noted, there is always a place at which the person can redeem himself. If,

43

however, this process is never ended, the results are literally disastrous. They led Judas to betray his Master. They led the Romans to slaughter innocent Christians. And daily they lead otherwise moral, decent people to acts of hate, revenge, and evil, allowing them, moreover, to justify these acts with a sense of inner perfection, thereby hiding the image of God and further staining the fallen man.

Of the person who cannot overcome false humility and *plane,* St. John Cassian tells us much in his discussion of errant, proud monastics. Such a person begins to think himself superior to his spiritual advisors. Everyone becomes false in his spirituality, practicing a distortion. He begins to think that, because his inner perfection has been revealed to him, his sins are incidental. He begins to judge others, accusing them of judging him. A sense of spiritual elation grows in the person, alongside a desperate anguish which drives him from hearing any spiritual words and listening to any spiritual counsel that might cure him. He begins to think that all others are unworthy, and their apparent unworthiness becomes a justification for his growing hate, envy, and jealousy. He finally comes to such a state that he is unable to tolerate the spirituality of others. He cannot bear to listen to their words. He becomes an open servant of evil, often even fabricating his own religion, his own prayers, and his own rule of conduct. And the great tragedy that ends this is that he not only separates himself from those who are spiritual, but those who are spiritual must separate themselves from him. As St. John Cassian comments, spiritual men begin to receive the words of these poor demonic victims as "words uttered from Lucifer himself." Such is the frightful consequence of false humility.

HUMILITY AND THE FUTURE OF ORTHODOXY

As the Orthodox world faces the onslaught of modernity, it finds itself where it has never been before. If, in the past, the Church was beset by enemies, they were enemies of a different kind than those whom She encounters today. The great heresies of the past were heresies which distorted the Christian truth, which distorted the path to God, yet acknowledged the existence of truth. Today, however, there is a universal, world-wide denial of truth itself. In the past, arrogant Christians took it upon themselves to define the Church as they wished it to be, to appropriate the infallibility of the Ship of Salvation for an individual, an institution, or a man-made theological system. Today, having cast themselves into the sea of disbelief, men deny the existence of such a ship; and those, indeed, at the helm of that ship have lost all sense of their duty to guide her responsibly. In ages past, living always with an apocalyptic spirit, ever anticipating the appearance of Christ, Christians lived in constant fear of God. In this century, when the inevitability of a nuclear holocaust or environmental disaster makes the apocalyptic imminent, the spiritual is of secondary import. In such conditions, it is absolutely imperative that we re-capture the mind of the Fathers, that we prepare ourselves and our world for the spiritual transformation that may soon befall all of mankind. It is imperative that we know our Orthodoxy with a depth never before known, since what threatens us is unique and ominous. And to know what we must, we must acknowledge what we have lost. And to acknowledge what we have lost, we must humble ourselves in all ways. We must begin our great ascent towards the spiritual imperative of our age with utter meekness.

2

HUMILITY AND THE SPIRITUAL WORLD OF DOSTOEVSKY

By Sister Paula

The remarkable depth of Russian literature, in the opinion of many Russian and non-Russian critics, is nowhere more ideally expressed than in the novels of Dostoevsky. This is partly because Dostoevsky combines, in his writing, a deep understanding of human psychology with the sensitivity and spiritual insight of his profoundly Orthodox soul. However, it is more precisely because his spiritual world is permeated by the union of mind and spirit bequeathed to him by his Orthodox heritage. This union is revealed in the universality of his characters, who are richly personal, real humans who play out their lives along transcendent spiritual dimensions. For Dostoevsky, where there is no spirit, there is no person; where there is no God, there is no man.

In the following essay, Sister Paula discusses the spiritual world of Dostoevsky so magnificently captured in his perhaps most accomplished work, The Brothers Karamazov. *We see, in her treatment of this novel, his penetrating understanding of a humility of mind and spirit which emerges only from the Orthodox Patristic tradition, a tradition that assuredly touched the genius of Dostoevsky.*

The genius of the great Russian *littérateur*, Feodor Dostoevsky, lay in a peculiar combination of the realist and the idealist, the sensuous and the spiritual, in which these divergent tendencies were almost equally matched. Whatever havoc this may have come to wreak on his personal life, in his art it permitted him to absorb the conflicting, often hostile philosophical and social trends of his day and to transform them into novels of consummate artistry and perceptive insight. Moreover, the dualism of Dostoevsky's nature was, as he assuredly knew himself, one of the keys to his ability to see and to expose the subtlest motivations and workings of human thought and feeling. It was, indeed, a spiritual insight of sorts, bringing to him an intimate knowledge of the debauched and the saintly, the abandoned and the scornful, opening their inner lives to him. With his peculiar grasp of the intricate interworkings of the mundane and the spiritual, Dostoevsky understood, better than their promulgators, the ramifications of the avant-garde ideas of his day. He embodied the abstractions of nihilism and atheism in such characters as Raskolnikov and Stravrogin, showing precisely the spiritual annihilation inherent in the ideas they voiced, yet retaining, in his trenchant exposition of their passions and personal pathos, the vividness of art.

Few of Dostoevsky's novels are more complex, more prophetic, or more expressive of his peculiar spiritual vision than *The Brothers Karamazov*. At its publication, it took Russia by storm, and Dostoevsky himself considered it the capstone of his career. In it, perhaps more than in any other of his writings, he gives flesh to all that he knew and felt about God and man, the nature of society, and the true ends of human pursuit — particularly the true ends of the vogue socialism and nihilism gathering such great strength in the Russia of his day. *The Brothers Karamazov* captures a Dostoevsky who knew the frailty of the human and the imperative nature of the divine, the struggle between the debilitating power of pride and the transforming quality of humility. To understand fully the true import of the book, and Dostoevsky's intentions in writing it, is to know the man, to understand the personal experiences which formed his mind and spirit.

Dostoevsky wrote and published *The Brothers* very near the end of his life, after returning from abroad and re-establishing himself in Petersburg. The years spent abroad with his wife Anna and their children left an effect which may well be judged from a letter written by Nicolai Strakhov:

[The years abroad] . . . were in the best time of his life . . ., the time which yielded the most profound and the purest thoughts and feelings . . . . [He] lived almost exclusively in total solitude . . ., remote from all occasion to deviate from the straight path of development of his thinking and his profound spiritual work. The birth of children, concern for them, the sharing of man and wife in one another's suffering, even the death of his first-born — all these were pure, sometimes exalted experiences. There is no doubt that it was precisely abroad . . . that the particular revelation of the Christian spirit which had always dwelt in him was consummated.

This fundamental change was revealed very clearly . . . when Fyodor Mikhailovich returned from abroad. He would constantly bring the conversation around to religious themes.Not only that; his manner changed, acquired greater mild-ness sometimes verging on utter gentleness. Even his features bore traces of that frame of mind. . . . It was evident that the highest Christian feel-ings dwelt in him . . ., which were expressed in his work ever more often and distinctly. This was the man who returned from abroad.[1]

The Dostoevsky who came back to Petersburg was indeed much changed. He was to change even further during and after the death of his young son, Alyosha, in Petersburg. His tremendous grief at this was in large part the impetus for his pilgrimage to the Optina monastery and his talks with Staretz Amvrosy. Under the influence of his long isolation abroad, his sorrows, and his intui-tive understanding of the most complex moral and psychological disorders, Dostoevsky began to bring his worlds of realism and idealism, of the sensuous and the spiritual, into concord, into that deep blending of the world and God so typical of the Russian Orthodox soul.

His masterpiece was taking shape, emerging from the maturity of his own spirit.

The Brothers Karamazov is nominally a book about the murder of old Karamazov. In reality, however, it is a polyphonic essay about pride and humility, about the final antipodes of life which Dostoevsky's spiritual journey had so clearly revealed to him. And it is around these two poles, pride and humility, that everything in the book is arranged. Dostoevsky always wrote around an "idea," making one or more comments about man and society (whether Russian or European), but bringing these observations back to an essential point. Of his ideas in *The Brothers Karamazov* he writes the following to Liubimov:

> [The idea of the fifth book] . . . is to depict extreme blasphemy and the seeds of the idea of destruction which exist in our time in Russia in a milieu of young people who have lost touch with reality, and also to portray . . . their anarchy. It will also include a refutation of these things . . . in the last words of the dying Elder Zosima. . . . These modern convictions are precisely those which I would accept as a synthesis of modern Russian anarchism. There is a denial, not of God, but of the meaning of His creation. The whole of socialism grew out of an initial denial of the significance of historical reality, and it has now arrived at a program of destruction and anarchism.[2]

Of Father Zosima Dostoevsky tells Liubimov:

> The next book will contain the death of the Elder Zosima and his conversations with his friends before he dies. . . . If this is a success I will have done something worthwhile: *I will force people to admit that a pure, ideal Christian is not an abstraction but a graphically real being whom [you] encounter face-to-face, and that Christianity*

is the sole refuge of the Russian land from all her woes. I pray to God that it succeeds; if it only has enough inspiration, it will have a moving effect. . . . The whole novel is written for the sake of this theme.[3]

If Dostoevsky showed prophetic powers in his view of the future of Russia as he set about writing *The Brothers,* he had equal insight into the pride of a society which sought order without God and which had, as its only hope, the virtue of Christian humility. That Dostoevsky had such visions is disputed by most critics, both in the West and in the Soviet Union, who find in his "ideas," as expressed to Liubimov, an apparent desire to mollify the imperial censors by being as Tsarist and as Orthodox (*i.e.,* as "reactionary," in their minds) as possible. The folly of these critics is affirmed by reading the novel itself. One cannot help but believe that Dostoevsky meant what he wrote about his intentions in producing the novel. His own understanding of the struggle between pride and humility, between the arrogance of those who think to find a utopian society in human weakness and the meekness of those who await the coming of the Divine Kingdom — this understanding is the very image from which Dostoevsky draws his contrast between anarchy and order. This understanding is the cornerstone of his novel. It reveals both the depth of his work and the spiritual accomplishment of his soul, the grasp of the two ultimate poles of life-experience which had somehow developed from his peculiarly dualistic genius.

By the time that he began *The Brothers,* the choice between pride and humility, order and anarchy, sin and repentance, and the consequences of that choice were clear to Dostoevsky. His work was to embody that clarity and bring it to focus on the problems of his beloved Russia. Metropolitan Antony (Khrapovitsky), the émigré Russian theologian and brilliant commentator on the novels of Dostoevsky, argues precisely that Dostoevsky's works were not imbued with intentions other than those which we see so lucidly put forth in *The Brothers Karamozov*. The "all encompassing idea" of Dostoevsky's writing, Metropolitan Antony writes, "was not patriotism, not slavophilism, not even religion in the context of a collection of dogmas, but repentance and regeneration, falling into sin, and correction, and if not that, then embittered suicide."[4] Dostoevsky, indeed, brought to his work the ominous choice between pride and self-destruction and humility and regeneration.

It is through the Karamazovs that Dostoevsky makes his most compelling statement about pride and humility, about rebellion and obedience. In them he personifies the struggle between these universal opposites. The lines are succinctly drawn between the camp of the proud and that of the humble. In fact, each character, from the onset, is described in terms of relative pride or humility. Some, like Dmitri, begin in pride and end in humility. Others, like Alyosha or Ivan, know where they stand from the first; yet even for them, there is a precise and manifest moment of choice when a decision must be made between rebellion and obedience. Their humility is not a fixed thing, but a lived trait. To be sure, all of the sorrows and evils portrayed in the book stem, in one way or another, from pride. And all of the peace and genuine love depicted in the book flow from loving humility.

All of the proud characters in the book know, indeed, that they are proud. Whether or not he admits it to others, at some point each admits it to himself. Pride, being a deliberate reduction of the world to its impression on oneself, is, naturally, habitually self-conscious.

But Dostoevsky takes pains to show that a mere admission of pride is quite insufficient for redemption, or even improvement. Ivan, Katya, old Karamazov, Mitya — all of them admit their pride, or are forced into admitting it by others; only Mitya, however, finally escapes the tyranny of ego. In Mitya, Dostoevsky shows clearly that, for an admission of pride to be salutary, it must be accompanied by a correspondingly vivid awareness of divine humility and personal responsibility in the face of that humility. One must see, deeply and profoundly, that the life of pride has been a conscious alignment of one's will with the forces of spiritual rebellion and destruction. One must see both the purity and the humility of God, feel them as active forces, and respond fully to the responsibility of internalizing and activating them in one's own life. In essence, an awareness of pride is curative only in proportion to the clarity of one's vision of God and the sincerity of one's surrender to Him. Where no vision or confession of God exists, awareness of pride serves only to reinforce one's sin and egotism. A recognition of rebellion, without an agreement to surrender, only crystallizes, finalizes, one's defiant rejection of God.

The paths of the proud and the humble way may be easily traced in the novel. Abstracted and distilled, the opposing roads may be "mapped" in four steps. The regenerative road of the humble begins in a spiritual, noumenal vision of God, of His goodness and humility, which leads to reflection on one's moral irresponsibility and imperfection. Coming in this way to a new, rather painful, self-knowledge, the penitent sees the depth of his rebellion, the true magnitude of the hatred of God and man into which his pride has led him, and through this begins attaining some small part of the love, faith and humility which lead him to regeneration and redemption.

The destructive road of the proud begins in a stubbornly materialistic, egocentric view of life and the world, a view which ignores or rejects God entirely. In this deliberate blindness, the proud man makes himself and the world in the image of his own ego, painting flattering portraits of himself and generating groundless theories of life. Comfortable, or at least sovereign, in his self-made, self-interpreted world, he refuses to accept the validity of external moral standards or internal moral promptings (which might tend to undermine his ego-centric freedom). He is led farther and farther into blindness and self-deception. Shrouded in his spiritual blindness and self-will, he may reach a point where he will find the eternal pain of rejecting God preferable to the transient pains of self-abnegation, the loss of his ego more fearful than the loss of his soul, and so slides freely into destruction.

Everyone in *The Brothers Karamazov* follows one of these two paths; regardless of individual differences in the distance traveled or the point reached, for the Karamazovs, as for all men, there are only two choices — rebellion or obedience. The antipodes of those two choices are typified in the Karamazov Patriarch and in Staretz Zosima; everyone else in the novel is traveling toward the archetypical humility of the Staretz or the supreme pride of old Karamazov.

Fyodor Pavlovich, that most unpaternal of patriarchs, as befits an embodiment of rampant pride and rabid ego, is a man of no redeeming qualities whatever. He wants money, women, life itself, only because he *wants*, not because he appreciates any intrinsic beauty or worth in these things. An utter materialist, he is the ultimate consumer, lacking any sense of discrimination. For him everything exists to be ingested, as much and as quickly as possible. In the manner of a small and greedy boy grabbing candy in both hands, cramming full his mouth and all his pockets, trampling what he can't carry away, old Karamazov may not want everything he takes; but it is imperative that no one else gets it. He knows he is hateful and nasty and is driven even further into outrageous vileness and slander simply from an acute, though unrepentant, sense of his own baseness and moral leprosy. Instead of repenting and reforming, he wishes only to avenge himself on the witnesses of his buffoonery and debauchery.

Having chosen, early in life, to devote himself to

egocentrism and self-indulgence, Feodor Pavlovich kept resolutely to his course in spite of occasional, but unmistakable, inner promptings to the contrary. Through continual moral license and indulgence, he dims and finally stifles all intuitive memory of a higher life, and becomes the definitive example of what pride can make of a man. He participates to the fullest possible extent in the metaphysical force of pride, and in return is transformed into a goitered, wattlenecked lecher whose brains are beaten out by a man who is the direct product of his immorality.

In Father Zosima the reader is offered the other end of the road, a man who participates to the fullest possible extent in holiness, whose transformation is directly wrought by humility and follows precisely the paradigm outlined above.

As a young officer of independent means, he too began in rebellion and self-indulgence. If not potentially another Fyodor Pavlovich, he was at least an energetic traveler on the same highway, until his pride led him into a manufactured rage and an unjust duel. The night before the contest, while in a "savage and brutal humor," he beat his orderly for some trivial error and awoke feeling "vile and shameful."[5] Upon reflection, he discovered that it was not the coming duel, but the vicious beating of his servant that oppressed him so.

He experienced, at that moment, the pivotal realization that is the first step on the road to humility: the suddenly awakened awareness of the goodness and humility of God. Inspired by his new sense of God and of his own error and moral guilt, he at once begged forgiveness of his servant, resigned from the regiment, and finally entered a monastery. He set out on a course designed to teach him that nothing is less important (or, indeed, more harmful) than his own whim, a path in which he is made free of his own desires and, in refusing to fulfill them, actually satisfies the deepest longing of his heart — the wish to regain and develop the original purity and holiness natural to man. He abandons his money and his ambition, abases himself and lives in penitence, immerses himself in the metaphysical dynamic of humility, and is transformed into a regenerated, enlightened man whose spiritual purity and attainment make him a channel for the regeneration of others.

All the plots and subplots of the novel only further illumine the battle between pride and humility (or, more fully, between rebellion against, or obedience to, God). Whether one considers the havoc wrought by the domestic tyranny and vain pride of a woman such as Katya, or Ivan's "elevated" intellectual crises and suffering nihilism, or Dmitri's profligacy and temper, the groundnote of all their various agonies is still pride.

The difference between Dostoevsky's approach to his thematic contention between pride and humility (the approach of an eminently *Orthodox* writer) and that of a Western artist is quite significant and deserves consideration. In this difference lies a key to Orthodox perceptions of pride and humility, of culture, and of the individual's responsibility in the face of his culture, all of which are regarded quite differently in the West. Regardless of whom one examines, these differences are manifested starkly and inescapably throughout *The Brothers Karamazov*. If one considers an existential, nihilistic rebellion such as Ivan's, what is in the West a majestic rebellion against a God who cannot "give an account of Himself" — epic material rich in pathos, full of sadness and dignity, the finely chiseled beauty of a Miltonic Satan —, is, in the Orthodox world, reduced to its true significance and horror: an aging lecher stiffening in a pool of his own blood and an embittered, sickly epileptic dangling from a rope in a roach-infested room.

Our possible shock or twinge of disgust at such a comparison is ample evidence of our complicity in, or contamination by, the glorification of rebellion endemic to our culture. It is we who err, who exaggerate, who distort; we, not Dostoevsky, are lulled by the romantic trappings of pride and anarchy. Our culture is in many respects a monument to the subtlety and skill of demonic deceptions capable of making us think Satan heroic and rebellion noble.

The choices are clear. Dostoevsky knew and understood the spiritual forces at work in the hearts and minds of men, the ravenous malignity of pride and the demonic force of rebellion, the divine force of humility and the saving strength of obedience — and his portrayal of their effects on human lives is convincing and convicting. Even, at times, terrifying.

It is a serious error to regard Dostoevsky's portrait as only a novel, however great, and ignore the spiritual profundity that makes it a work of genius. Literature was never meant to be the sole preserve of academics and specialists, but rather the voice of a people. At its best, it can be a teacher and corrector of the people, and it is this role Dostoevsky can play best for us. We face the same spiritual nets that winnowed the Russian people; their blindness and coldness are now ours. We must not look away from our own faces in the Karamazov gallery; old Karamazov is as clear an indictment of our evasions and self-deceptions as it was for Dostoevsky's first readers, and the Staretz is as firm a promise of what we could become. The choices facing America in the 1980s are substantially those which faced Russia in the 1880s, for each man in his day must choose between Karamazov and the Staretz.

The Brothers Karamazov warns the West especially clearly, for our entire culture cries out against the humility and self-abnegation of the Staretz. If Russia, a country steeped in Orthodox ascetic spirituality, could become so full of devils and Karamazovs by 1917, what can one hope for in an America where humility is so un-American? Inheritors of a monolithic materialism, children of an age of unparalleled hedonism and selfishness, our position is indeed perilous. Our culture is rooted in apostasy and self-indulgence; our lives are dominated by a cult of success and worldliness (far greater threats to spirituality than any mere paganism ever was). We teach our children from birth to rely upon themselves, to follow their own ambitions and desires, to get ahead in the world as quickly and as far as possible. We judge others (and ourselves) by the quantity and quality of our possessions, and have even become so apostate as to think, and to preach, that financial success is a sign of God's favor, that suffering or privation are indicators of divine displeasure or, at best, disinterest. If our children cry out against our materialism, our selfishness, our smugness, we call them cultists or fanatics, urging them to avoid getting too caught up in God, lest they fail to accumulate more cars and clothes.

All of these attitudes were antithetical to Russian culture in its truest form, and yet Russia became captive to a terrifyingly powerful spirit of atheism and materialism, whose fruits are too well known to need mention here. The bitterness that may await an America whose social ethos is predicated on materialism and egocentricism is even more frightening.

We face yet another trap of pride, one that perhaps not even the Karamazovs faced, a trap infinitely more subtle than atheism or nihilism. An atheist or a nihilist knows that he rejects something, and may even know (at least dimly) what he rejects. Now, in our age, for the first time a man can be trapped and destroyed by his best and highest impulses, his religious nature, if he is not remorselessly honest. He can destroy himself with what he thinks to be Christianity; proudly, if innocently, secure in his heresies, he can stroll calmly to perdition, despising and mocking true Christianity and thanking God for his new car.

Dostoevsky's Russia had preserved the spiritual ladder

of Orthodoxy, by which man climbs out of himself into the refuge of humility, for nine centuries, and still Dostoevsky warned them of their danger. What would he say to our world, a world in which men have never seen a true ladder, tap together bits of lath, and proudly carry their spindling toys into appalling spiritual danger?

Now, when as never before we face personal and cultural catastrophes that can only be survived by the soberest humility and the deepest trust in God, the West ignores the only sure means of acquiring that humility and trust, thinking to arm itself in the tatters and rags of heresy, of sects too limited (when sincere) and too bankrupt (when not) to provide a good defense against the unsleeping malignity of old Karamazov's master.

We are indeed a nation of Karamazovs. The heady, exuberant sweetness of our success has been heavy in the air a long time, but now an even heavier, sweeter smell is beginning to creep around us. It is impossible to pretend that the smell of our cultural decay will just go away; we cannot remove it by any manner except one. We too must enter the fire; whether that fire will be a metaphysical one, or a horrifyingly real one, is only a matter of time and choice. For now, we may still have a little time to choose the metaphorical, spiritual purgation.

Orthodoxy is truly a living image of one crying in the wilderness of this lunatic cacophony, surrounded by materialists who call Her outmoded and heretics who call Her heretical! For us, as for the Karamazovs, She waits patiently with the ladder of humility and self-abnegation that is our only escape from the tyranny of egos and possessions. Both roads are open to us; we may follow our cultural leanings, as old Karamazov followed his personal desires, or we may deny ourselves and our culture, and take up the Orthodoxy that has created innumerable Father Zosimas.

Whatever we choose, it is wise to remember that the fruits of our choices wait for us, as Karamazov's did for him; our creations are patient — well able to wait; but they never sleep. The forces that sweep through the lives of the Karamazovs are as active today as ever. The demonic tide of hate and anarchy that reached a peak in the destruction of Russia and the martyrdom of the Church may have fallen a bit, but it assuredly lies in readiness to flood again. Then, as always, there can be but one refuge: the humility of Christ engendered by Orthodox spirituality. If not in ourselves, then we may at least find in Dostoevsky's spiritual world a hint of that humility. Today, as in his day, Dostoevsky's literature evokes a spiritual nostalgia, a desire for an abundant life that calls us, across all of the Christian centuries, to the lofty heights of lowliness.

Dostoevsky dealt with real problems and forces, and we in turn must examine his work, and our experiences, in the light of these forces. To regard such concerns as outside the province of criticism is to force art outside the province of life. Art is not something divorced from reality, but reality itself, heightened and illumined, and must be protected constantly against sterile academic interpretations. In reading Dostoevsky, we must keep one eye on his world and one on our own, constantly juxtaposing and comparing these two worlds. If we fail to do so, we make warnings useless and his solutions empty — we compromise the universality of his themes.

His picture of an old, crippled monk preaching the Gospel of Righteousness and the Kingdom of Love, and winning in his struggle with the world, strikes an unaccustomed note in our more enlightened, more sensible world; such an image may seem to us outmoded, even faintly ludicrous. His portrayal of men and women tormented and finally destroyed by their own pride may seem, to our egocentric sensibilities, theatrical or excessive.

We would do well, before dismissing Dostoevsky's art as merely art, before refusing to recognize our own likeness to his Karamazovs, to reflect soberly on the final scenes of the novel. In the end, the last triumphant note is sung by the humble, and from the proud comes only the silence of sorrow and death. Such is the spectacle of spiritual life reduced to the struggle between the proud and the humble, which so shines in Dostoevsky's literary — may we say theological? — genius. And such is the portrayal, we secretly know in our hearts, of all life.

NOTES

[1] Anna Dostoevsky, *Reminiscences.* Trans. Beatrice Stillman (New York, 1975), pp. 169-70.

[2] Vladimir Seduro, *Dostoevsky's Image in Russia Today.* (Belrnont, Mass., 1975), p. 195.

[3] *Ibid.,* p. 196.

[4] Metropolitan Antony Khrapovitsky, *Dostoevsky's Concept of Spiritual Rebirth.* Trans. Ludmila Koehler (Chilliwack, B.C., 1980), p. 12.

[5] Fyodor Dostoevsky, *The Brothers Karamazov.* Trans. Constance Garnett (New York, 1950), p. 355.

3

THE DESERT FATHERS ON HUMILITY

Translated from the Greek By Archimandrite Chrysostomos and Father Theodore M. Williams

The Euergetinos contains rich spiritual lessons which still speak to us across the centuries. These lessons are neither theological nor personal: they are not theological, for they describe more than theory — they describe theory in practice; they are not personal, for their universal significance rises above the individual. In all that one might write about humility, nothing so adequately captures the virtue as the Euergetinos, wherein is found a living, breathing humility. The following anecdotes, aphorisms, and tales from the desert Fathers, therefore, are an apt summary for our few, hopefully instructive words on this virtue of virtues.

"I prefer a humble fall to a proud victory," one Father says.

* * * * *

And Abba Sarmatias said:
"I prefer a sinful man, who recognizes his fault and humbles himself, to a self-complacent man of virtue."

* * * * *

"Humility, without great effort, has saved many," another elder says. "This is evidenced by the tax collector and the prodigal son, who, with the few humble words that they spoke, were received by God."

* * * * *

"The woman from Canaan spoke and was heard. The woman with the issue of blood remained silent and was blessed. The tax collector dared not open his mouth and was justified. The Pharisee cried out and was condemned," said Abba Epifanios.

*　*　*　*　*

"Before any other thing, we have need of humility," St. Isaias the Anchorite writes. "Let us be ready, in every circumstance, immediately to say 'forgive me' to our brother. Humility destroys every snare of the devil."

*　*　*　*　*

And another Father said:
"A humble person humiliates the demons. A proud person is mocked by them."

*　*　*　*　*

Abba Iperechios calls humility the tree of life, which rises up to loftiness.

*　*　*　*　*

All of the Fathers call humility the monk's crown.

*　*　*　*　*

A certain Father was asked when a man attains humility. "When he remembers his sins continually," he replied.

*　*　*　*　*

"Just as the ground on which we walk has no fear of falling," a certain elder said, "so is the humble man."

* * * * *

"He who first asks forgiveness, though another offends him, has true humility," another Father says.

* * * * *

One of the Fathers was asked what he considered true progress in man.

"Humility," he answered, without hesitation. "The more the soul descends into profound humility, the more it ascends to all the other virtues."

* * * * *

"When the passions cease to battle us," the Fathers say, "we must then humble ourselves, so that God, Who knows our weakness, can protect us. If we boast that we are controlled, He immediately takes away His Grace and we are then once more taken over by passions."

* * * * *

A certain hermit, who used to wear just a hair shirt, went to Abba Ammonas to confess.

"That alone will benefit you in nothing, brother," the elder told him, pointing to the hair shirt.

"I am troubled by three thoughts, Abba," the hermit said. "One tells me to live very deep in the desert; the other, to go as an unknown stranger to some faraway place; and the third, to shut myself away in my hut, without seeing a person, and to eat only every two days. Which do I choose from all of these?"

"None of them will benefit you," the elder answered. "If you wish to hear my advice, stay in your cell, eat a little each day, and keep the words of the tax collector always in your mind and in your heart: 'God, be merciful to me a sinner.' You will find salvation only in humility."

* * * * *

A young man went to Abba Theodoros of Fermi to tell him his troubles.

"In the world I fasted ever so much, Abba. I observed frequent vigils, I had contrition and tears in my prayer, and I had in my heart a great passion for every act pleasing to God. Here in the desert I have lost all of these things, and I fear that I will not save my soul."

"That which you did in the world, my son," the wise elder told him, "was nothing more than a work of vanity, for human praise. God did not accept it. There in the world, the devil did not battle you, nor did he impede your eagerness, since it brought you no profit. Now, however, that you are more decisively enlisted in the army of Christ, the devil, too, has armed himself against you. You must learn that one psalm said with humility here in the desert is more pleasing than the thousands that you said there with vanity; moreover, the Lord receives more gratefully the one day of fasting that you do here secretly than the many entire weeks of fasting that you did in front of others in the world."

"I do nothing now," insisted the youth. "I was better there."

"It is arrogance," Abba Theodoros sternly told him, "that you still think you were better in the world. The Pharisee in the parable had the same opinion of himself, and he was censured. Say, my child, that you have never accomplished any good. It is in this way that the tax collector was justified. The sinner with a broken heart and humble thoughts is more pleasing to God than a proudly virtuous man.''

The elder's lesson, replete with practical experience, brought the young monk to his senses.

As he was saying farewell and leaving, he gratefully told the elder: ''Thanks to you, elder, I have today saved my soul.''

*   *   *   *   *

The Bishop of a certain province once fell into great sin. The next day was a Feast Day, and he was supposed to Liturgize at a Church that was celebrating its Patron Saint and to which the whole city usually went.

As soon as he entered the Church, he went up on the *ambon,* revealed his sin in front of the crowd, took off his episcopal stole, gave it to his Deacon, and with great contrition said loudly, so that all could hear:

''After such a sin, I can no longer be your Bishop. Choose someone worthy.''

He started to leave. However, the people, who loved him, prevented him.

''Remain in your post and let the sin be on us,'' they all shouted with one voice.

Moved by the love of the people, the Bishop once again ascended the *ambon* and said:

''If you want me to stay in my post, which I hold unworthily, you will do as I tell you.''

He ordered the doors of the Church shut and only one small exit to remain open. He fell to the ground in front of the exit and shouted to the congregation for all of them to listen to him:

''Anyone who dares not step on me, when leaving here, will have no place with God.''

The Christians, in order not to lose their Bishop, obeyed. One by one, as they left, they stepped on him. When the last one had passed, a voice from Heaven was heard saying:

"Because of his great humility, his sin is forgiven."

*   *   *   *   *

"I once saw all of the snares of the devil spread across the earth," St. Antonios the Great said, "and I became frightened."

"Who could possibly escape them?" he wondered, sighing.

He then heard a mysterious voice answering him:

"He who is humble."

*   *   *   *   *

While yet a young monk, Abba Pimin asked to learn from Antonios the Great what he should do to find his salvation.

"Acknowledge your faults with a contrite heart," the Father of Fathers answered him, "and humble yourself before God. As well, endure the trials which befall you patiently, being sure that God will save you."

*   *   *   *   *

Great temptations once beset St. Arsenios. One day the brothers heard him praying with these words:

"My God, I, the unworthy one, dare to beseech you not to leave me alone in my affliction. I know that I have done nothing in my life which has been pleasing to Thee, but Thine infinite mercy can help me in beginning anew."

*   *   *   *   *

An industrious young man traversed the desert for some days, in order to meet Abba Ammois and to consult with him. The elder kept him with him a whole week, but said nothing during this entire interval. When the youth was finally preparing to leave, the kind Father followed him to the door and then told him these words:

"My sins, my child, have become a high wall which separates me from God."

The pious youth thanked the holy elder and left, benefited by the elder's great humility.

* * * * *

The daughter of a certain rich man in Alexandria was suddenly seized by a wicked spirit and was suffering horribly. The father spent a great deal of money to make her well. To no benefit, however. The young girl's condition became worse and worse. Somehow, he learned that a hermit, living the ascetic life up on a mountain, had from God the gift to cast out demons. He was told, however, that the hermit was so humble that he would never agree to perform such a cure. It was, therefore, necessary for the nobleman to find some other pretext by which to get him to his home.

One day the hermit went down to the city to sell his baskets. The father of the girl sent a servant to buy some and to ask the hermit home to be paid. Unsuspecting, he went. The moment he put his foot inside, however, the demonized girl, who was hidden behind the door, jumped on him and gave him a hard slap on the face. The saintly hermit, without at all losing his composure, humbly turned his other cheek, fulfilling, in this way, the commandment of the Lord.

Then this surprising thing took place: The demon began to tremble wildly and to give forth desperate cries:

"O hurry! I am leaving. I cannot remain any longer. The commandment of Christ is casting me out."

With these words, the tormented creature was set free. All of the family, together with the girl, who had now regained her senses, glorified God for the great miracle they had seen with their own eyes. Then they looked for the holy elder, in order to thank him. He, however, that he might flee human praise, had completely vanished.

When the Fathers in the desert were informed of these facts, they said among themselves that nothing so exhausts the pride of the devil as humility and submission to the divine commandments.

*   *   *   *   *

Abba Karion frequently confessed to his fellow ascetics that he had labored more in asceticism than his son, Zacharias, but had not yet succeeded in reaching the stature of his son, who was adorned by two great virtues: humility and silence.

One night, when Zacharias was still very young, nearly a child, he fell into ecstasy and saw a divine vision. The next day he revealed it to his father. The father, however, like the practical man that he was, scolded and chided him, telling him that all such things were errors and demonic fantasy. Yet the child continued to be more fervent in his prayer and to receive divine revelations. But since his father did not want to listen to him in any manner, he decided to visit Abba Pimin.

The Saint carefully listened to the boy and, seeing him aflame with divine love, understood how the Grace of the Holy Spirit had come upon him; however, for greater assurance, he sent the boy to consult the most experienced of the elders there.

Zacharias did as Abba Pimin told him. Before he had time to confess, though, the experienced elder revealed the youth's thoughts to him:

"Divine Grace has come upon you, my child," he told him. "However, return to your father and submit yourself to him humbly, so that he remains in your heart."

The youth faithfully followed the direction of the Saint

and benefited.

*   *   *   *   *

Abba Moses asked the young Zacharias:

"What can I do, my child, to be saved?"

"You ask ignorant me, Abba?" he told him shyly.

"Believe me, brother, I saw the Holy Spirit overshadow you and this compels me to take your advice."

So Zacharias took his monastic cap from his head, threw it on the ground, and began to trample on it, saying:

"If the monk is not trampled on in this manner, Abba, he does not find salvation."

*   *   *   *   *

God quickly called this same earthly angel near him. During his last moments, many great Fathers of the skete had gathered around him. Among them were Abba Isidoros the Presbyter, St. Pimen, and Moses the Egyptian, who had a close spiritual relationship to the blessed Zacharias.

The dying youth had raised his eyes toward Heaven. It was clear that he was beholding only the incorporeal world.

"At what are you so persistently gazing, child?" Abba Joseph asked from time to time, barely able to control his tears at the loss of his little friend.

"Is it not preferable that I am silent, Abba?" he whispered.

"Yes, my child. You have always preferred humble silence."

When he finally died, his face sparkled, such that it had the look of an angel. Abba Isidoros, who was standing silently at one side, raised his tear-filled eyes toward Heaven and murmured:

"Rejoice, child Zacharias. The gates of Eternity are now being opened for you."

* * * * *

Theofilos, the Patriarch of Alexandria, set out to visit the ascetics of Nitria. On the road, he encountered an elderly ascetic.

"What have you gained, Abba, living in this isolation?" the Patriarch asked.

"I have come to know myself well," the elder replied, "and I have learned to reproach myself."

"It is impossible for a man to accomplish a greater feat in his life," the Patriarch admitted.

As soon as he reached the skete, the Fathers came out to greet him, and each one found some good word to tell him. Only Abba Pambo stood to one side, silently.

"Are you not going to say something beneficial to the Patriarch?" the elders asked him.

"If he does not benefit from my silence, brothers, then neither will my words occasion him profit," the wise Father replied.

* * * * *

"The beginning of man's salvation," writes Evagrios, "is accurate knowledge of himself."

* * * * *

Abba Theodoros of Fermi once sat down to eat with the brothers and noticed that they drank water without first asking that the blessing be given, as was the ancient custom among monks. The elder sighed deeply and said:

"The monks of today have lost their politeness."

* * * * *

A certain brother asked the same Abba Theodoros what to do in order to keep the divine commandments always.

"My fellow ascetic, Abba Theonas, had exactly the same desire," the elder answered, "so listen to what he did: He went to the oven one morning to bake his loaves of bread. Just as he was taking them out, freshly hot, a couple of beggars happened by. Without hesitating, Abba Theonas distributed all of the loaves to them. Returning to his cell, he encountered other beggars on the road and, since he had no more bread, he gave them his baskets. Farther on he found someone naked and took pity on him. He immediately took off his clothing and dressed him. Arriving at his cell naked himself, the Abba reproached himself anew, saying:

"'Woe is me. I never keep the commandments of God.'"

* * * * *

A certain other brother went to Abba Theodoros in an agitated state:

"Help me, Father," he pleaded, "my soul is being lost."

The elder sadly shook his head:

"I am myself in danger, my child," he told him, "and you seek strength from me?"

His humility, however, was sufficient to benefit the brother.

* * * * *

St. Theodora had the custom of telling her disciples

very frequently that neither great asceticism, nor extreme toil, nor any other hardships whatever can save the soul of man so much as humility of heart. And she would relate the following anecdote:

A certain hermit had the gift from God to expel evil spirits. Once he asked to learn what they feared most and what would force them to flee.

"Maybe fasting?" he asked one of them.

"We," answered the spirit, "neither ever eat nor drink."

"Vigils then?"

"We do not sleep at all."

"Fleeing the world?"

The demon laughed contemptuously: "Supposedly an important thing. But we spend the greater part of our time going around the deserts."

"I abjure you to confess what it is that can subdue you," the elder insisted.

The evil spirit, compelled by an other-worldly power, was forced to answer: "Humility, which we can never overcome."

*   *   *   *   *

"Higher than all the virtues," Abba John the Short used to say, "stand the fear of God and humility."

He once asked one of his visitors who it was that he thought sold Joseph [the Comely].

"His brothers," the visitor answered.

"No," the elder said. "His great humility. Do you not suppose that, at the time they were selling him, he could have protested and shouted out that he was their brother? He remained silent, however, and allowed them to give him to the merchants. This humility of his made him a nobleman in Egypt."

Again another time he said:

"What fools we men are. We cast the lightest burden, the admission of our faults and the words 'forgive me,' far from us, yet take on ourselves the heaviest burden, self-justification."

The same Abba John was so humble that the Fathers of the skete continuously said of him:

"By his humility, John the Short has suspended the whole of the skete from his little finger."

*   *   *   *   *

Heed what Abba John the Thebite says of humility:

"Before all other virtues, the man of God must attain humility. This the Divine Teacher pointed out to us first. 'Blessed are the poor of spirit,' He told us, 'for theirs is the Kingdom of Heaven.' And who are called the poor in spirit? Surely they are the humble."

*   *   *   *   *

"The more that a man approaches God, so much more he considers himself wretched," Abba Matoes tells us. "The Prophet Isaiah, when he was found worthy to behold the Lord of Glory, called himself paltry and unclean."

Yet another time he told the brothers:

"When I was young, now and then it passed through my mind that I had done something worthy of note. Now that I have grown old, I see that I have done nothing noteworthy."

*   *   *   *   *

"How was it that many of the ancient Fathers succeeded in fulfilling the divine commandment of humility, Father?" a certain brother asked an elder.

"Behold their example, how they loved their enemies more than themselves," he replied.

"Woe unto me, such an unfortunate man! Not even those who love me do I love more than myself."

* * * * *

Abba Iakovos once went to visit Abba Matoes and told him how he planned to visit and to speak with all of the Fathers in some particular desert.

"Greet Abba John for me," the elder asked.

When Abba Iakovos reached Abba John, he conveyed to him the greeting of Abba Matoes.

"Matoes," Abba John joyfully said, "is indeed an Israelite without guile."

After some time, Abba Iakovos again went to see Abba Matoes and related to him the words which Abba John had said about him.

"I am not worthy of such praise," Abba Matoes humbly replied. "But learn this, brother: When a man honors his neighbor more than himself, he has attained to a high degree of virtue."

* * * * *

Once while counselling a brother, Abba Matoes said to him:

"With fervent prayer, my child, ask two things of God: To grant you saving contrition in remembering your sins always and to place humility in your heart, so that you think yourself worse than all men and so that you never judge another.

"Flee accursed boldness in speech and control your tongue as much as you can. Do not be a disputant in arguments. If the person speaking with you says something correct, agree with him. If not, do not argue with him, but say, 'you know best, brother.' All of these are signs of humility."

* * * * *

A certain brother wanted to know the meaning of self-reproach.

"To think yourself worse than the dumb beasts," Abba Alonios explained to him, "who have the good fortune of not having to account for their deeds."

* * * * *

"My dog," Abba Isidoros once said, "is in a more fortunate position than I. For he has love and will not have to justify his deeds."

* * * * *

St. Pimin said of Abba Isidoros, the Priest of the skete, that he passed the greater part of his life stooped over his handiwork. The brothers begged him not to torture his body so.

"If I were taken and burned alive," he told them, "and my ashes thrown to the four winds, this sacrifice would have no meaning before the boundless sacrifice which the Son of God made on my behalf."

Once when he was beset by the thought of boasting of a certain virtue he possessed, Abba Isidoros said to himself:

"Could it be that you possibly consider yourself an Antonios the Great or the equal of the Abba Pambo or the other Fathers, who found such favor with God?"

Another time the devil tried to cast him into doubt by murmuring in his mind that, despite all of his labors, the Abba had not succeeded in saving himself, and would be condemned to eternal hell. He answered the devil angrily:

"And if I go to Hades, devil, I will have you underfoot."

* * * * *

"When a man learns to reproach himself, in whatever circumstance, he has the power to endure," Abba Pimin often said.

Yet another time he said:

"In order to understand the Scriptural passage, 'unto the pure all things are pure,' a man must think himself worse than all creatures."

"How can I think myself worse than a murderer?" a certain brother asked.

"By saying to yourself," the elder explained, "that a murderer has committed only that one sin, while in my thoughts I *daily* kill my fellow man."

* * * * *

"One who has learned to accuse *himself*," says Abba Anoub, "finds it easy to excuse the faults of another."

* * * * *

All of the Fathers acknowledge the humility of Abba Pimin in his every behavior. For example, when he conversed with the elders, he never advocated his own view. He always gave way to and honored the opinions of others. The brothers who went to seek his counsel he always sent to his older brother, Abba Anoub. And Abba Anoub would, in turn, send them back to Abba Pimin, telling them that God had given to the Father the grace to comfort souls.

Before his older brother, Abba Pimin never opened his mouth to speak to anyone. He would stay to one side with his head bowed, out of modesty and reverence.

* * * * *

"We can discern goodness of character in a man," St. Antonios said, "when he admits his faults and endures until his last breath all temptations which befall him."

Another time, sighing, he related this:

"In this hut you will find every virtue, save one. And how, without that virtue — how am I, unfortunate as I am, to make progress?"

"And what virtue is that?" the brothers asked.

"Self-reproach," replied the great Father.

* * * * *

"I will go to the same place to which the devil is condemned," said St. Pimin, humbling himself.

Yet another time:

"Man has as great a need for humility and fear of God as he does for the air he breathes."

Again, in another instance:

"The most useful tools of the soul are humility, self-reproach, and contempt for one's own will."

* * * * *

Once all of the elders of the skete were eating at the common table. Abba Alonios, being young as he was, stood aside and served them. The Fathers spoke praisingly of him. He lowered his head humbly, without responding at all.

"Why did you not speak, Abba, when they spoke well of you?" one of the brothers who happened to be nearby later asked.

"If I had spoken," he answered, "it would have

indicated that I accepted the praise, whereas in fact my soul despises it."

* * * * *

A novice monk asked Abba Pimin to teach him how to rest in his cell.

"I, my son," the Saint told him, "examine myself well within the silence of my cell, finding myself a sinful man plunged up to my neck in the mire of dissoluteness and laden with an unbearable burden. Thus I never cease crying with all my soul to our All-Merciful God: 'Lord have mercy upon me.' The monk who unceasingly has God before his eyes and stays in his cell with reverence and modesty will not fall into any serious sin."

"If a particular brother whose company is not beneficial to me happens to come to my cell, what am I do to?" the monk asked to know.

"Examine yourself well," the Saint advised him, "to see what your thoughts are before the brother visits. You will discover that you are to blame for this lack of benefit and that the circumstance is not created by someone else. If you do this always with true humility, you will not judge your neighbor, but only yourself."

* * * * *

A certain monk told Abba Sisoes in confidence that he had at last succeeded in keeping his mind unceasingly fixed on God.

"This, my child," the discerning elder told him, "is neither a great feat nor one of your own making, but is from Divine Grace. A great thing is to think yourself worse than all men. This is called *HUMILITY*."

* * * * *

78

St. Sisoes once passed the hut of a certain anchorite, greeted him, and asked how he was.

"Look how I squander away my time," the anchorite replied.

"How blessed it would be if I, too, could squander away my time without amassing sins," the humble elder said, sighing.

*   *   *   *   *

Three hermits once travelled from far away to find Abba Sisoes and to speak with him. Each of them had some perplexing problem for him to resolve.

"How will I escape the river of fire?" the first asked.

The elder heard him but did not give an answer to him.

"I am wondering how I can be saved from the gnashing of teeth and the unsleeping worm," the second hermit commented.

Abba Sisoes did not reply to him either.

"What can I do, Abba, since the thought of the outer darkness allows me not even a moment of peace?" the third hermit asked.

"I, my brothers," the elder then said, "never think of any of these things. I only hope that the mercy of the Lord will save me."

The hermits, upset that their perplexities remained unresolved, stood up to leave. The elder then told them:

"You are indeed fortunate, my brothers, and I am surely envious of you. With the thoughts that you hold, it is impossible for you to fall into sin. But alas, as for me, it never occurs to me that there is a hell awaiting mankind and I heedlessly sin every moment."

*   *   *   *   *

"The way leading us to true humility," the same Saint said, "is in sobriety, prayer, and self-denial."

Yet another time, he said:

"The Holy Scriptures tell of idols that: 'they have mouths and do not speak; they have eyes and do not see; they have ears and do not hear.' O, if only the monk could be so! Besides this, the idol is also considered an abomination. Let the monk, too, think himself an abomination, in order to save his soul."

*   *   *   *   *

Abba Kronios considers the fear of God to be the means by which the soul is guided to real humility.

*   *   *   *   *

A certain holy elder, once seeing the devil with his own eyes, boldly asked him:

"Why do you war against me with such perseverance?"

"Since you resist me with your constant humility," the devil replied, becoming invisible.

*   *   *   *   *

As St. Makarios was returning to his cell one day, carrying palm leaves for his handicrafts, the devil stopped him, ready to assault him. He could not. An insurmountable force prevented him.

"You have annoyed me greatly, Makarios," the devil fiercely yelled. "I have warred against you for so many years, yet I cannot take you. Indeed, what greater things have you accomplished than I? Perhaps fasting? But I never eat. Vigils? I do not even have need of food. You have only one fearsome power that frightens me."

"What is that?" the Saint asked with great interest.

"Humility," the devil unwillingly confessed and disappeared.

*   *   *   *   *

"Why does the devil war against monks with such passion?" the brothers asked a spiritual elder. "How is he so bold?"

"If monks would immediately put forward their defensive weapons — humility, poverty, and patience —, the devil would never dare approach them," the elder replied.

*   *   *   *   *

"Do not make a habit of humble speech," another elder counsels, "but of humility of mind. Without humility one is unable to make progress in spiritual things and to observe the Will of God."

*   *   *   *   *

Two brothers fled to the desert and pursued the ascetic life together in the same hut. The devil, envious of their love, set about to separate them.

One evening the younger brother, in going to light the oil lantern, upset it and spilled the oil. The elder brother became angry and slapped him. Then the younger brother, without being disturbed by this, bowed, made a prostration, and humbly said:

"Forgive my carelessness, brother. I will immediately make ready another lantern."

The same evening, a pagan priest who chanced to be in his temple heard demons holding a tribunal among themselves. One of them confessed with embarrassment to his leader:

"I went and put the monks in consternation. But is it my fault that one of them turned to the other, made a prostration to him, and destroyed all of my work?"

Hearing these things, the pagan priest straightforward became a Christian and withdrew into the desert. For the whole of his life he guarded his heart with humility and unceasingly had ready at his lips the words, "forgive me."

* * * * *

Some Christians from the Thebaid brought a certain demoniac, bound in chains, to a hermit elder, that he might make him well. The holy elder commanded the evil spirit to go out from the creature of God.

"I will not go out," it cried out, "unless you first tell me who the goats and the sheep of whom Christ speaks are."

"I am one of the goats," answered the elder. "As for his sheep, He is the one who knows them."

"Your humility casts me out," cried the frightened demon, and he went far away from the unfortunate man who had been so tormented.

* * * * *

Speaking of humility of mind, a certain wise elder said the following, which is worthy of note:

"When you make a prostration before your brother and humbly ask forgiveness, you immediately expel every operation of the evil one against you. The miller places blinders on the eyes of the animal which turns the mill, so that it will not turn and eat from the product of its toil. Let us also do the same. Placing the blinders of humility over our eyes, we will not see our few good works and thus not grow proud and lose the product of our toil.

"Provided that through them we reproach ourselves, sometimes God allows impure thoughts to attack us, that we should not be high-minded. Such thoughts are, to some extent, coverings over the little good that we might have by chance accomplished. He who continually reproaches himself does not lose his reward."

*   *   *   *   *

A certain brother asked one of the great elders to define humility.

"Humility, my child, is always to understand yourself as sinful and worse than all men," explained the elder. "This is a great and difficult achievement. However, applying yourself in incessant toil, you can obtain it."

"But how is it possible to see yourself continually as the worst among all?" the brother mused.

"Learn to see the good qualities of others and faults in yourself, begging forgiveness for your faults from God each day, and you will succeed," advised the Saint.

*   *   *   *   *

A young monk attained to such humility that he said only these words in his prayer to God:

"Lord, cast lightning down on my head and wipe me from the face of the earth, for as long as I live I disobey Thee."

*   *   *   *   *

A certain irritable man, once blinded by the passion of anger, attacked a certain Christian without reason. The injured man, almost choking in his blood, made a prostration before his murderer and humbly kissed his hand, saying to him:

"I was in the wrong, brother, forgive me."

*　*　*　*　*

One very humble Father in a certain coenobitic monastery, faithfully following the exhortation of the Apostle, "bear ye one another's burdens," would himself take responsibility when any of the monks did wrong, accusing himself and thankfully receiving the punishments imposed on him.

The other monks, however, not seeing the virtue of the brother, but rather some awkwardness in his handiwork (he was a bit slow), constantly spoke against him and said amongst themselves:

"Look how he always makes so many mistakes and how he is good-for-nothing."

But the Abbot, knowing how virtuous the brother in question actually was, told those speaking against him:

"I prefer one of his mats, woven with humility, to however many you fashion with pride."

One day the Abbot once more caught the monks speaking against the monk for his clumsiness. He took the baskets which they had woven from them and tossed them into a fire burning in the middle of the compound. Along with them he threw the basket of the humble brother. Shortly, all of the baskets became ashes, save that of the humble brother, which the Abbot took unburned from the fire.

Seeing this miracle, the monks, so given to condemnation in the past, made a prostration before their humble brother and asked his forgiveness. From that time on they honored him as a spiritual Father.

*　*　*　*　*

Abba Longinos was once asked what virtue he

considered the most important of all. The wise elder replied:

"Just as pride is the greatest of all evils, since it succeeded in casting down the angels from Heaven to the abyss, so humility is the greatest of all virtues. It has the power to raise the sinner from the abyss up to Heaven. For this reason, the Lord blesses, before all others, the poor of spirit."

*   *   *   *   *